DPA Dominique Perrault Architecture

Maria Vittoria Capitanucci

DPA
Dominique Perrault
Architecture
Recent Works

SKIRA

Cover
New Mariinsky Theatre, Saint Petersburg
Velodrome, Berlin
Town Hall of Innsbruck, southern façade of
the central tower by Peter Kogler

Editor
Luca Molinari

Art Director
Marcello Francone

Editing
Francesca Ruggiero

Layout
Paola Ranzini

Translation
Lorenzo Sanguedolce, Language Consulting
Congressi S.r.l., Milan

First published in Italy in 2006 by
Skira Editore S.p.A.
Palazzo Casati Stampa
via Torino 61
20123 Milano
Italy
www.skira.net

Printed and bound in Italy. First edition

ISBN-13: 978-88-7624-269-4
ISBN-10: 88-7624-269-4

Distributed in North America by Rizzoli
International Publications, Inc., 300 Park
Avenue South, New York, NY 10010.
Distributed elsewhere in the world by
Thames and Hudson Ltd., 181A High
Holborn, London WC1V 7QX, United
Kingdom.

A special thank you
goes to the studio DPA
and particularly to architects
Astrid Rappel and Luca Bergo,
to Luca Molinari;
to Gabriella Capitanucci
for her invaluable new research.
This volume is dedicated to her.

The panels were prepared by
Gabriella Capitanucci (G.C.)
Graziella Germano (G.G.)
Carla Morogallo (C.M.)

Contents

Introduction
Maria Vittoria Capitanucci

Through certain protagonists of the architectural panorama, it is possible to interpret the cultural channels, the problems, the crisis and the afterthoughts of entire generations. Dominique Perrault, born in 1953, undisputed (yet oftentimes discussed) protagonist of international architecture, could represent, in this sense, a case study on a condition that concerns an ample portion of professional architects, particularly European and specifically French. Personalities of varying fame, completely inside and completely against the Star System, but all involved in the eighties in the spasmodic research of an architectural quality that was not completely oriented around isms postmodernism for starters, followed by deconstructivism and also minimalism —and of a language that allowed for specific connotation. Successively, the nineties gave rise to a generation who trusted in the instrumental value of the contest —preferably public— in hopes of intervening in the great urban transformations of contemporary metropolises; still later, they found themselves wrapped up and involved, utterly impotent, in the great economic and cultural crisis, destined to persist through the present day, causing a reduction in the number of assignments and interventions, yet simultaneously spawning an intensification of theoretical value in planning and of participation in opportunities of public and private contests. Perrault, through a completely personal procedure, not at all comparable to other members of his generation, traversed these moments with light movements and interventions, accepting to distance himself, as concerned his planning, from Paris[1], where he had had the initial opportunity to express himself with the grandeur of the Bibliothèque nationale, but also with France, a territory that is spangled with his remarkable interventions —the Esiee, the Center for Book Treatment, the Departmental Archives of Mayenne or the Aplix factory would suffice— so as to begin concentrating on Europe.

Looking back for a moment, it may become clear how this distancing came about. Regarding the French condition[2] at the end of the eighties, J. Lucan wrote that 1983 marked the end of the wave of contests for large projects, but at the same time, in a climate of strong reexamination, not excluding the political realm, following Socialism's defeat in the municipal elections, Mitterrand turns his attention to themes such as those of the Banlieu, the repossession of the suburbs and degenerated areas, of which the reconversion of the Halle de la Villette[3] would play an emblematic, pioneering role. This marks the point of departure of a renewed interest in the problems concerning construction and materials, already introduced through the matrix of prestigious Anglo-Saxon personalities based in France, such as Peter Rice, the structural and engineering mastermind behind the

9

mythical Beaubourg —whose influence "through a curious phenomenon [...] did not immediately manifest itself"— as well as Richard Rogers, Renzo Piano and Norman Foster. "The fashion of high-tech architecture must have a determining influence on the most recent production of young architects such as Christian Hauvette, Dominique Perrault, Francis Soler and the group Architecture Studio who, having abandoned all inclination for competitions, dedicate themselves to planning buildings with smooth, abstract surfaces and profiles of aluminum, metal and glass, which leave little to the imagination regarding the volumetrics and the interior spaces, giving the general impression that the decision to hide reinforced cement has been forgotten. This high-tech "French way", which now has an essential point of reference in a building such as the Institute of the Arabic World, aspires to a different image from modernity, metaphorically close to that offered by industrial products. And, as if by a strange vendetta of history, it seems to attach itself, in some cases, to certain characteristics of the international style, forgetting the tenor of the debates of recent years[4]". The words of Lucan, although charged with bitter polemic and implying a negative judgment of this new generation of planners, to whom he merely refers in passing, conduct us to a series of reflections on the methodological choices, both in planning and in composition, of an entire generation.

It remains a curious fact that Lucan has indicated, for example, 1988 as the chronological limit to his own analysis, when the contest for the Bibliothèque nationale was held just one year later, the last of the great projects sponsored by Mitterrand in preparation for the bicentennial celebration of the French Revolution, to which he dedicates an entire paragraph in his volume[5]. It would therefore be appropriate to reflect on whether this vision is still acceptable in light of what was to come.

Perhaps it is not quite true that these professionals simply abandon contextualism, a theme that would continually remain a priority, foundational and present, in the work of Perrault, who graduated from the school of Antoine Grumbach[6], founder of the Groupe des sept[7] and one of the protagonists of the theorization of "urban architecture". On the other hand, Lucan's description of the materials and elements of this architecture, although purely descriptive and based wholly on aesthetics, is certainly an accurate one, regarding a research of the absence of materiality which, however, does not necessarily, equal, as in Perrault's case, a desire to supersede or hide the structural skeleton, the reinforced cement. Finally, one should examine where and in what sense the concept of "French style" high-tech is hidden within the folds of architecture, as the French critic indicates; an overly naïve vision that has little relevance to Perrault's work: perhaps in the fascination of the Hotel Berlier and its system of plant design, or in the cultural machine represented by the Esiee, or rather in the four towering sheets of the Bibliothèque, or in the industrial buildings and athletic facilities? All of these are occasions in which high technology does not correspond to a high structural tenor, where the pleasure of returning to a certain severity of material and form brings us closer to the Brutalism of the Smithsons than to the Lloyd's of Rogers. But it is valid, even if not entirely correct, the intuition according to which Perrault and "the others" (but who are these "others"?) approach the International Style: they premeditatively pursue a break in the hyper-theoretical academism of their fathers. It is true that American Mies —and perhaps also Gropius— is present in DPA's work; *less is more* could be one of his slogans if it were not for the fact that his works are continually permeated by vision of the location's geography and based on the use of geometry as a planning instrument. In particular, the grid theme, present in numerous projects of both urban and territorial design —imagine the contest-project for the Falck area in Sesto San Giovanni, or the Mitra Temple in Naples— as well as in the composition of constructions —from Aplix to the Bibliothèque's glass walls, from the Hotel Berlier or the Town Hall of Innsbruck to the Library of Kansai Kan— as Laurent Stalder wrote, "it is simultaneously a structure and a method of the architectural idea. And inevitably, it is also the generational origin of form"[8]. But this fascination with geometry does not have an exclusively positivist or rationalist matrix and it is easy to trace its origin in Conceptual Art as well[9].

Beyond his declared passion for the world and the theory of art, Perrault's tendency towards a contamination of arts, particularly on themes of urban, landscape and territorial design in general, is evident. The strong and ever-present influence of Land Art, a current of conceptual art that his procedures, methods and, of course, his conceptuality grasp with positivist pragmatism, is frequently traced in his work.

Just as Frédéric Migayrou is, for example, in his essay published in the monographic issue of "El Croquis", in speaking of "La Violencia de lo neutro"[10], of a minimalism that is never a style or a simple formal will in Perrault, but is rather closely tied to the radical hopes of the seventies as a need to reexamine an alternative to formalist and historicist architecture. Therefore, it would be an error to continue to associate his work with that of the minimalists when he himself, on multiple occasions, has declared to consider this architectural current, a successor of postmodernism and deconstructivism, as a moment of "absence", ready to transform itself into a linguistic renewal. Asked of his admired artists, he referred to the work of Bruce Nauman and of James Turrel[11], undisputed protagonists in the artis-

Plans for the Kansai Kan Library

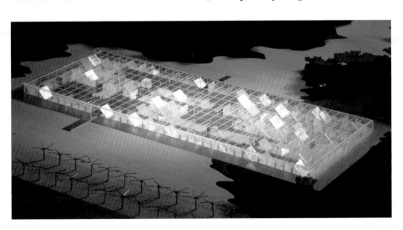

tic panorama but, although close to conceptual art, certainly distant from the minimalist positions of the United States. Thus, even recently, Perrault has sought the collaboration of Daniel Buren[12] in his projects on more than one occasion. Contamination among the arts, which is certainly not limited to a citation of Carl André or the Land Art of Richard Long, even though the reference to the latter tendency is evident in projects intended to mark the territory, such as the very conception at the base of the program for the athletic area in Berlin, or the rocky strip for the renovation of the beach of Tenerife, or even its trace in the fascinating sinuousness of the planar curves, like a crystallized, geometric volcanic crater upon which the Cultural Center of Santiago de Compostela is constructed. Marks upon the territory that penetrate it and artificialize it remain dazzled, frozen in time, as if every aspect of dynamism were interrupted for an immeasurable period. Flows, on the other hand, regain their dynamic charge, such as in the recent proposals of the important series of international contests, which features, among others, the new Congressional Center in Rome, the new headquarters of the Pinault Foundation and the Mariinsky Theatre, along with the High-speed Station of Afragola and the restructuring of Piazza Garibaldi in Naples. These are all projects that seem to be fueled by a new energetic flow, a vital sap that seems to move through the "resulting spaces" complex multifunctional systems, elevated to true public spaces, whose role assumes a foundational value for the entire program.

Apparent Neutrality and Possessing the Location
In Perrault's projects, beginning with his earliest, there is always an evident tendency to possess the location through the architectural object, as occurs with the penetration of the territory, never fearing the hypogeal construction, which is always represented on the surface by a visible presence, as in the Bibliothèque nationale of Paris, with its forest and towers; as in the platform, which unfortunately remained only a plan, for the Library of Kansai Kan, with its three gardens (naturally, of reading crystal); as in the prismatic and reflective sheet, installed on top of the Cultural Center

of Santiago de Compostela; and as in the slit characterizing the recent Ewha Campus in Seoul. Also a strong appropriation is that occurring in the Esiee, where the long perspective loses its direction, inclining and becoming a surface in which completely reinterpreted views are created, resulting in a new relationship with the location.

But it is in the Velodrome and Swimming Pool of Berlin, where the buildings are practically eliminated, disappearing into the earth, that an ulterior, new aspect comes to play —the claiming of public space through the definition of a skin that is separated from the structure yet remains strongly connected. It is that interstitial space between the metallic net and the infinite glass wall that surrounds the entire perimeter of the Swimming Pool and Velodrome. It is the pale and slightly detached covering, *alla* Christo that wraps the project for the new Center for Contemporary Art of the Pinault Foundation; it is the golden motif enveloping the Mariinsky Theatre like an antique cupola or crown.

An aspiration to the artificialization of landscape that always joins in the emphasis of the location's outline, of its characteristics and its history, an attention to what is present as well as to what is not.

And here, another theme close to the heart of French architecture comes into play —absence, emptiness and transparency that can be summed up in "an almost nothing, or I don't know what"[13]. The theme of the large, transparent parallelepiped container periodically returns in Perrault's production, practically incarnating the concept of *non locations* introduced by the French anthropologist Marc Augé[14] and later borrowed in the criticism of contemporary architecture.

Minimalism, large containers and absence are all powerfully returning themes in Perrault's work. A symbol among them is the Hotel Industriel Jean-Baptiste Berlier (Paris, 1986-1990), which also houses the headquarters of Perrault's studio and is the result of a contest that slightly anticipated the more famous one for the Bibliothèque nationale, in a nearby area of the same arrondissement (XII). Emblematic of the concept of *non location*, as insinuated by his own definition, "Hotel Industriel" —not even trans-

ESIEE (University for Electric Engineering) in Marne la Vallée: comprehensive view with the central traversing gallery, detail of entrance

latable in Italian— this building proposes itself as the interpretation of a space without specific quality or destination, emptied, none the less, for a special flexibility that does not classify it in the productive or in the tertiary sector. But it is primarily a luminous lantern in the night of the first peripheral ring of Paris, a transparent and dimmed presence by day, never the same, but nevertheless a conspicuous landmark for a large number of cities due to its shameless positioning between the entrance to the Quai d'Ivry and the railway lines entering the city. It is with this building that Perrault introduces a theme, or rather a typology in absence of specificity, which is that of the container, preferably prismatic. Consider the four towers of the Bibliothèque nationale de France, the closed and introspective "grilled" fronts of the Departmental Archives of Mayenne, the anonymous, metal balloon-frame system of the Centre Technique du Livre in Bussy Saint-Georges, and finally the algid Media Library of Venissieux, which are no more than empty bodies purposely and premeditatedly conveying an apparent neutrality, far from the dialectic architecture of Kauffmanian[15] memoir of the "revolutionary" architects Ledoux, Boullée and Lequeu, they are all interventions that favor a relationship with the territory rather than self-representation.

The Aplix institute in Le Cellier-sur-Loire (1997-1999) is emblematic of this quality, a reflective line on the French countryside, balancing between a Robert Morris installation[16] and crossword puzzle design in which each square measures 20 x 20 meters. A game of reflections and deformations that makes

The Hôtel Industriel Berlier in Paris: nocturnal view and corner detail

Departmental Archives
of La Mayenne: detail
of the extension of the
historic building
and the covering within
the reading room

the intervention of the following year (2004) unique —in another industrial plant, manufacturer of metallic mesh for Gdk Usa in Cambridge, Maryland. Here, despite the geometrical disposition of the building's layout, the theme of the mirrored surface makes way for a modulated skin of a "metallic" quality, in line with the research of recent years expressed in the relationship with context and between interior and exterior.

An apparent neutrality is conveyed by the Perraultian containers, which seem to be related to a concept introduced by Hans Ibelings in writing of a new "ism" —*supermodernism*: "After postmodernism and deconstructivism, a new manner of conceiving and creating architecture seems to emerge: a manner that is largely indifferent to the concepts of location, context and identity worshipped by postmodernism in its impertinent attempt to resume the past. With respect to the cult of postmodernism for ornamentation and memory, supermodernism is characterized by a sensibility for neutrality, for the undefined, the implicit and the tendency towards an idea of space as a controlled emptiness"[17]. This position was also taken by Fulvio Irace, who in fact, in his *Dimenticare Vitruvio*, adds the following to this supermodern thread: "a tendency brought to the top by a younger generation of artists, such as the Swiss Herzog & de Meuron, the French Nouvel and Perrault, the Dutch Wiel Arets and Rem Koolhas, the

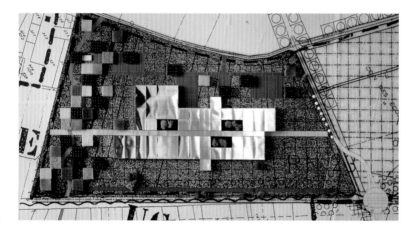

Aplix Plant
in Le Cellier-sur-Loire:
model, front corner detail
and interior view

American Staven Holl and the Japanese Toyo Ito and Kazuyo Seijma"[18]. But how much affinity exists among these protagonists? Undeniably, they are related through a purely generational kinship as well as an experimentation of the potential and of the use of certain materials, but in actuality, is the fluctuating transparency of Ito's *blurring architecture*[19] traceable in Perrault's work?

In Perrault's most recent productions —with a single paradox, confirming the continual modification of architectural language as represented by the M-Preis chain of supermarkets in Austria, which perhaps personifies the idea of hyper-location[20]— it is as if this concept of apparent neutrality, which is no longer the same as *non location*[21], has become focused on a precise circuit, elevated towards a theme, a typology, that of tall buildings —towers— whose destination is unknown, yet whose presence is constantly perceived as a conspicuous point in the city's horizontal fabric. Such is the case in the skylines of numerous urbanistic studies: that of the Viennese Danau City (2002-2006), towers soaring 200 meters high, of unknown destination, and a tower for habitation (of ninety units in Durango-Bilbao, 2004-2007) interspersed with skyscrapers for hotels (Tour-hotel, Habitat and Tour-hotel Castro in Barcelona, 2000) in the Spanish sky, as in the Japanese (Aomori Northern housing), sometimes even zigzag-

ging, as was planned for the Royaume-Uni in London, or skewed in the manner of the "trays" of Wright and Kahn and certain Deconstructivists in the plans for the New York headquarters of Vanity Fair and Amag-Bvk in Zurich.

Regarding an entirely different series of interventions (a large part of them for important contests) that have occupied Perrault in recent years, we can not neglect to evidence a branch of research that could once again be defined as a relation to collective space, but in an unprecedented sense in the complex panorama of Dpa's production.

Every example of his architecture is unfathomable if not as a composition, juxtaposition and sometimes permeation of fullness and emptiness, of transparency and opacity with a recent aspiration to the research of a third condition, as mentioned, which is that of a "non-specific" space, a perfect limbo for the suggestion of new systems —that of the Mariinsky Theatre, the Pinault Foundation, the Afragola Station, the athletic box of Manzanares Park— with a concept not yet evident in the complex, dichotomous program of the Bibliothèque nationale or the Court of Luxembourg, but which arrives with delicate arrogance in the project for Berlin; that is why the Velodrome and Swimming Pool mark the ideal point of departure for this journey through the recent works of Perrault. Despite the fact that the Berlin contest dates back to 1992, its entire process being realized then, the appropriation of the context characterizing the facilities and the compositional choice to penetrate the territory as well as the definition of a "third road" in terms of collective space, makes this project the manifesto and the beginning of a research, which leads to the introduction of the new millennium and, for this reason, it can legitimately incarnate, because of its foundational and recurring themes, an opportunity for reflection on the most recent progress of French planning. From here on, Perrault plays with the resulting space, proposing it as a planned location and volume, protagonist of the transition between interior and exterior, between transparency and opacity, between specific and generic space. The French son of "less is more" of Mies van der Rohe, but closer to the German master of the Minerals and Metals Research Building of IIT in Chicago and of the Lake Shore Drive Apartments than to the author of the Barcelona pavilion, Perrault is never classical in terms of a trilithic approach to architecture, as was Mies with the Spanish pavilion. Despite the fact that he is continually fascinated by the very concept of the structural skeleton, he follows a rationalization of the planning process, passing through the skeleton by means of a compositional grill concept that is even reflected in the metallic scheme of the skin of his most recent buildings, woven like a "mat" rather than a structural element, curiously reproposing that uncommon and romantic union of Laugierian[22]-Semperian[23] dialogue.

Study for the tower of the Habitat Hotel Sky in Barcelona

[1] His studio has always remained in the suggestive space of the Hotel Berlier, the transparent prism a few blocks from the National Library, designed by him between 1986 and 1990.

[2] J. Lucan, *Francia, architettura 1965-88*, Electa, Milan, 1989.

[3] 1982-1985, work by Bernard Reichen and Philippe Robert, specialists in structural renovation of 19th century buildings.

[4] J. Lucan, *Francia, architettura 1965-88*, Electa, Milan, 1989, p. 180.

[5] *Ibid.*

[6] Grumbach, under whom he graduated, was among the protagonists of the theorizations on "urban architecture", well-known in the seventies for his studies conducted in parallel to the philosophers such as Michel Focault and theorists of architecture such as Bernard Huet and Bruno Fortier on the front of the formation and transformation of urban structures, dedicated to "invoking *an art to complete the city*" (A. Grumbach, *L'art de completer les villes*, in *Architecture en Frence, Modernité – Postmodernité*), a construction of the city upon itself, which refutes all clean sweeps, revalidating the proposal of Adolph Alphrand, the engineer responsible for the Haussmanian Paris.

[7] With J.P. Buffi, R. Castro, J.-P. Dollé, G. Naizot, G. Olive, C. de Portzamparc, all involved in teaching at the Pedagogic Unit of Architeture n. 6.

[8] L. Stalder, *Dominique Perrault. Progetti e architetture*, Electa, Milan, 2000, p. 12.

[9] The term "Conceptual Art", appearing for the first time in "Paragraphs on Conceptual Art" by Sol LeWitt (in *Artforum*, 1967), indicates an artistic tendency giving more importance to the concept, the mental process, than to the artistic object. In his text, Sol LeWitt sustained that in Conceptual Art, the idea or concept is the most important aspect of the work… the idea becomes a machine that creates art.

[10] Also the title of his essay in *El Croquis*, n. 104, 2001, pp. 258-260.

[11] See interview with Sebastien Redecke appearing in *Dominique Perrault*, Aedes, Berlin, 1996.

[12] Daniel Buren (Boulogne-Billancourt 1938), one of the most widely quoted contemporary artists in France, debuted at the end of the sixties with works in fabric, illustrated and colored in strips defined as "visual instruments". In time, his interests shifted towards three-dimensionality and the relationship with architecture in a study of modulation and mechanisms of space multiplication. In 1986, he represents France at the Biennial of Art in Venice and is awarded with the Golden Lion; in the same year, he completes the well-known installation Les deux Plateaux in the court of the Palais Royal of Paris and in 1995 in that of the municipal square of Lyon. In 2000 he is at the Spasimo of Palermo with *A cielo aperto*, a work in the degraded historical center. Perrault was involved on various occasions, including the plan for the new Town Hall of Innsbruck.

[13] Regarding the Hotel Berlier, in *Dominique Perrault*, London, 1994, p. 43.

[14] M. Augé, *Nonluoghi: introduzione a una antropologia della surmodernità*, Elèutera, Milan, 1993.

[15] E. Kaufmann, *Tre architetti rivoluzionari: Boullèe- Ledoux-Lequeu*, Franco Angeli, Milan, 1993.

[16] Robert Morris, key exponent of American Minimalism, who frequently used mirrors as a metaphor and as a material to refract mental discomfort.

[17] H. Ibelings, *Supermodernism. Architecture in the Age of Globalization*, Nai, Rotterdam, 1998.

[18] F. Irace, 'Dimenticare Vitruvio', *Il Sole 24ore*, Milan, 2001, p. 202.

[19] *Toyo Ito. Blurring architecture*, Charta, 2000.

[20] Category suggested by Aldo Bonomi. A. Bonomi, *Il distretto del piacere*, Bollati Boringhieri, Turin, 2000.

[21] M. Focault, *Eterotopia. Luoghi e non-luoghi metropolitani*, Mimesis, Milan, 1998.

[22] M.A. Laugier, *Essays sur l'architecture*, Paris, 1755.

[23] G. Semper, *I 4 elementi dell'architettura*, Italian translation, Jaca Book, Milan, 1991.

The Bibliothèque nationale de France. A Cultural Container between Medieval Abbey and Classical Temple

Not unlike William of Baskerville, the protagonist of Umberto Eco's *The Name of the Rose*[25], entering the monastery and the complex, symbolic and allegorical world of the library, so I attempt to penetrate into the theoretical and realizational program of Dominique Perrault, a world that is anything but labyrinthine, yet just as complex, sometimes presented cleanly and transparently as in his earlier buildings, towering on the urban periphery, sometimes implicitly and introspectively, like the ghosts of his enveloped and invisible masses, and other times intimately and attractively, like the bowels of the earth, which he penetrates without hesitation. The parallelism with Eco's well-known novel banally arises out of spontaneity when, analyzing Perrault's production, it is understood how the world of the book, in its ideal, cultural and real sense, represents a constant in his approach to architecture. Perhaps it is only a coincidence, but the young Frenchman's introduction to the "more structured" architectural panorama occurs with the Parisian Library. This, far from the gloomy, prohibited space of Eco's medieval Abbey, has its own symbolic composition made of its relationship with nature, which is a forest surrounded by a peripheral area, becoming in itself almost infinite in its irregular plot, and positioned upon a high podium with huge steps —not the podium of just any antique temple, but that of Apollo at Efeso, for example, one of the Seven Wonders of the World. Moreover, the Bibliothèque incarnates French grandeur, being one of the marvels desired by Mitterrand, and can legitimately be interpreted as a metaphor of philosophical research of truth —a constructive truth— almost classical, whose podium may be reached by means of the huge steps; a modern temple of contemporaneity, made of a four-part skeleton in turreted warehouse containers, in a continual relationship between full and empty that is a symbolic collective space, between transparency and opacity.

View of the Bibliothèque nationale de France, Paris

View of the Bibliothèque
nationale de France, Paris

Olympic Velodrome,
Berlin

Chapter I

Speaking of Architecture in relation to Public Space.
Six Cases at the turn of the Millennium

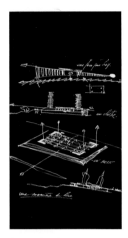

Study-sketch
of the Bibliothèque
nationale de France,
Paris

"As with the Bibliothèque nationale of Paris, Perrault has utilized a great volume to create a public space, a new urban landscape. The Velodrome and the Swimming Pool are underground: only their covers, a simple circle and a rectangle covered with tarps and metallic fabric, shine and reflect the light like extraterrestrial signals on the surface of our earth"[1]. The German critic, Redecke, in regarding the notable value of Dominique Perrault's Berlin project (for the Swimming Pool, he will have to wait a few more months) and of its role within the panorama of his architectural production, indicated, as is emblematic of the work, the definition of public space as its dominating theme, just as the case was with his most famous project, years before, the Bibliothèque. In this sense, the rare and essential gestures of the Velodrome and the Swimming Pool have led to a linguistic and compositional investigation, which continues today in the area of French architecture, continuously intended for the subjection to vast public exposure as one of the possible contextual variations, along with the complex relationship to its environment. Accessible spaces in the purest sense of the term: visually and practically, where the concept of "public" is not limited to the planning of well designed surroundings, or to an adequately congenial context, but is rather intrinsic of the work itself. In the case of Perrault's works, the opportunity to observe such a disposition exists in numerous occasions; the importance of the ring structure comes to mind, suspended upon *pilotis*, for the offices of the European Court in Luxembourg, which merges with the elevated position —as if a sacred "podium"— of the preexisting building, thus becoming a monument for the city; or the walkway from the Media Library of Vénissieux which, like a transparent telescope, visually connects two distinct urban areas: the square opposite the western face and the "wavy" lawn in front

Court of Justice
of the European
Community, Luxembourg

of the eastern. One element, already of strong presence in the Esiee, is the glass artery for distribution and crossing, which becomes a belvedere, a *passage* between the activities of the cultural center and the open spaces within it. Here, it is not only the transparency of the Media Library's fence which makes it resemble a jellyfish in the heart of the city, a location which clearly allows the perception of its presence without resulting in an invasive and egocentric display of material, nor is it the adequate redesign of the adjacent anterior square, paved and illuminated by Perrault's beautiful V-shaped lamps, nor is it the lawn, laid out between the Media Library and the Town Hall, but rather it is the system of relationships that is activated between all of these parts and the gallery, which eviscerates the enclosure of the Media Library without opening it. Such is, and perhaps even more so, the case with the Innsbruck Town Hall, whose project (1996-2002) recreates in the city's historical center a public square-garden readable only if viewed as the opening of the new municipal headquarters' space designated for events, a place of connection and transit, a center of coordination for a network of passageways and covered galleries leading to the city.

The trend of flow and visual relationships continues with the interior of the M-Preis chain of supermarkets, beginning with the Wattens I, where the green oasis, screen and scene between the building and the adjacent surrounding motorway, sinuously penetrates the algid and geometrically square glass surface of this "non-place", contemporary container of aliments. Recurring materials and themes, such as glass and steel, are the key to recognition for the other two projects also conceived for the Austrian chain, one being Wattens II, effectively a multipurpose box, even hous-

ing a post office within, and characterized by the penetration of public space —car park included— at ground level, through the transparent box's elevation upon pilotis. Here, the surface's transparency is accosted to the encompassing screen of a metallic skin, which regulates the infiltration of light through breaks and folds, marking the perimeter of the large commercial box, similar in vocation to the athletic box under construction in Manzanares Park in Madrid.

Lastly, in the supermarket of Zirl, a double construction comprised of one transparent body and one completely windowless (for service) the gestures are rare and determined. One of the glass walls, inclined in a diagonal orientation, provides a slice of interior space to that intermediate zone —not quite "external"— positioned in such a way as to relate to the exterior through a projected filter of green, while the completely flat overhanging roof, emphasizing the external public areas of shade and cover as it advances, mirrors the *parterre*, which surrounds the entire supermarket. Just a few gestures are able to define the capacity of a space to become public.

In conclusion, linear crack and penetration, generative elements already suggested, for example, in the project which competed for the Gallery of Modern Art in Rome[2], become one in the most recent of international competitions won by Perrault, the Ewha Women's University Campus in Seoul, where the feminine metaphor, never explicitly declared, seems to take form and, forging a new topography of the area, becomes a place of dispersal of currents, an urban space par excellence, hypothesis of complex relations and paths capable of reconnecting the university's preexisting structures with the neighboring city.

[1] S. Radecke, 'Velodromo, Berlino', *Domus*, 812, February 1999, pp. 12-21.
[2] Refer to chapter III, p. 146.

Velodrome and Olimpic Swimming Pool
Berlin, 1992-1999

The political ambitions of the Parliament, along with the desire to connect two parts of the city and a unifying project, the Olympic project, provided the opportunity for Berlin to develop a consistent number of athletic facilities and a new system of connection specially adapted to them.

In this context, in 1992, the city of Berlin, enthusiastic about the recent reunification, prepares an international public competition for the design of the Velodrome and Olympic Swimming Pool while awaiting selection for the 2000 Olympic Games.

The chosen area, destined to emphasize one of the city's most important entranceways from the east, is located at the intersection of two strong urban symbols: a major axis, ideally connecting Alexander Platz with Mosca, and a minor directional represented by the railway, which joins the city's east and west sides. Of the thirty-two participants, Perrault's project was chosen.

The Velodrome and the Swimming Pool thus create a new point of urban crystallization, a place for meditation between post-war constructions and the neighborhoods of nineteenth century industrial expansion, where the compositional choice was primarily focused on a "presence-absence", which even allows the two elements to disappear out of view. The project is based on the transformation of a vast rectangular area, within which two forms are inscribed, one round for the Velodrome and one rectangular for the Swimming Pool, according to the "primordial" figures of the two typologies. Two independent objects, simple in their composition, which defines a relation of pure proximity between them.

"The idea is to create a green space on an attractive scale (approximately 200 x 500 m), in whose center […] buildings are to be constructed. Athletic facilities of a high structural standard, with a skeleton in steel and reinforced cement, furnished with utilities and amenities without losing that sense of austerity intrinsic to sports, for all people, where the Velodrome presents a complex, self-standing ring for the covering's grid structure. For its diving boards, the Swimming Pool has a suggestive parallelepiped metallic grid, where, once again, the entire perimeter of the two geometric figures is surrounded by a double layer of metallic skin, interrupted in the lower section for public passage and access. A recess completely surrounds the two buildings, whereas an inclined escarpment allows them to be seen from above and permits a view of the surrounding green from the interior. In fact, the essential idea was to create an orchard by planting 450 apple trees with a history, so that their past could be traced, giving the green a sense of preexistence. German apple trees, naturally too regular, are not considered well adapted to the purpose and are "supplanted" by Norman trees, less uniform, but more resistant to transportation and above all to Berlin winters.

When approaching this orchard, one discovers, embedded in the earth, two surfaces —one round and the other rectangular— rising up one meter with their glass and metal coverings, dressed in thick webs of steel, sparkling like water in an urban park and, at night, luminous like landing pads for futuristic helicopters.

In contrast to the imposing stadium constructed for the 1936 Olympic Games in West Berlin, this open space in the urban fabric has assumed a more democratic and a more human symbolic value. "Architecture is antiauthoritarian". The work took second place in the 1999 Deutscher Architecturpreis.

This natural presence in the heart of the area between the Volkspark Friedrichshain, the Volkspark Prenzlauer Berg and the Sportforum Hohenschönhausen is a poetic response to its surroundings, which are today still marked by devastation and degradation. And, as in the case of the great public space of the Bibliothèque nationale de France in Paris, the relationship of these two buildings has represented an opportunity for redesigning the city.

The experience of arranging a public space in green for Berlin, an extremely interesting city from the point of view of its landscape, is a special one because it is the city where nature and architecture best mix. "And this mixture of nature and architecture is the kind of project that can be developed in the city… and particularly in Berlin". (G.C.)

General floor plan

Comprehensive view

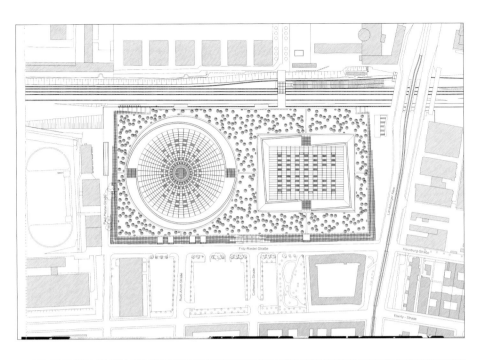

External detail of the
Swimming Pool: the green
penetrates the structure
through the metallic skin

Section of the Swimming
Pool

Interior of the Swimming
Pool: the hall

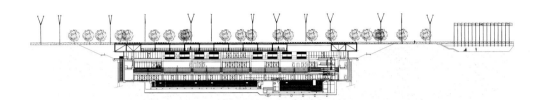

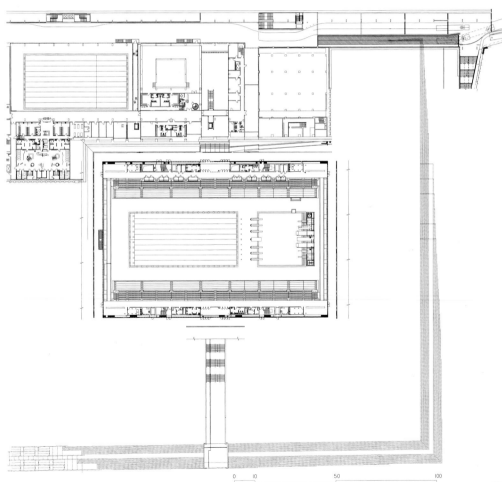

The Swimming Pool:
interior view with the
metallic "grid" trampoline
in the background

The Velodrome: interior
view; in the foreground,
the structure of the steel
covering

Detail of the Velodrome's
wrap-around front
and the access ramp
to the park

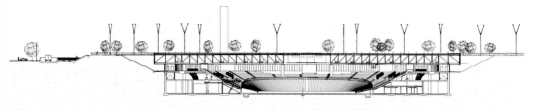

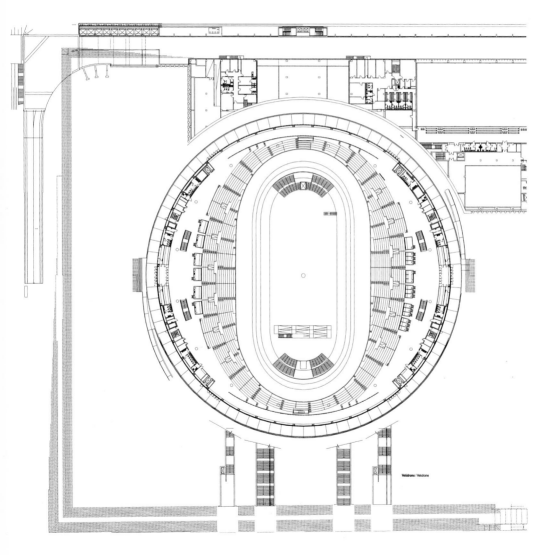

Velòdromo / Velodrome

Extension of the Court of Justice of the European Community
Luxembourg, 1996-2007

The construction of the tribune began at the beginning of the sixties, when the Kirschberg plateau was practically deserted, following an architectural contest won by Jamage & Van der Elste, from Liege and the Luxembourg Conzemius Group. At the end of 1978, the architect Bohdan Paczowski, active in Milan, and the Luxembourgers Fritsch, Herr, Huyberechts and Van Driessche were entrusted with the elaboration of a project for the extension of the old building, which stood out, isolated on an imposing base. They sought a solution that would respect its identity, while going along with the ensemble and taking advantage of the site's steep slope. The entire project was built upon the idea of strength inspired by the very nature of the city of Luxembourg. The proportionality of this design is still clearly interpreted today with regards to rapid circulation, large functional groupings and the crucial role of vegetation.

In 1994, as a reflection of the enlargement of the Union to new member States, the question of the reorganization and extension of the original building (100,000 m² of offices, rooms and services) was once again raised. Through an urban planning contest, a new commission was instituted for the Court of Justice, comprised of the Luxemburger studios Paczowski & Fritsch and Flammang & Lister. Dominique Perrault accepted entering the group, becoming the author of a project, which clearly expresses the idea of unification and interior opening, more than of a simple connection of juxtaposed elements.

The Court of Honor —the heart of the project— takes a leading role, a model for the development of all of the new functions requested. There are four phases in the planning of the work, each one corresponding to one of four architectural episodes. The first regards the existing building, stripped of its asbestos, of which the structure was conserved, along with the façade, furnished with a new skin. This space is dedicated to the new courtrooms, situated around a monumental stairway and the new lift systems. The offices, suspended on thin *pilotis*, envelop the historic nucleus in a quadrangular disposition, determining on the ground floor a portico area, almost classic, a thin filter between the exterior and the interior, but above all, an urban space utilizable independently from the functions of the tribune. A glass gallery unifies the ensemble, connecting the various functional areas and hosting services, such as the cafeteria and the library. Corresponding to this element, which would allow the connection of possible extensions to the east, is a passageway reserved for service vehicles. Across the vast church yard to the north, a privileged entranceway was created through a broad atrium beneath a ring-like structure. Finally, to mark the new city skyline, two towers designed to house offices, like blades, are inserted behind the courtyard of honor. Perrault subjects the existing complex to a ductile flexibility that conserves its rigor: it restitutes the center its primary role, focusing attention upon it to then distribute this concentration of energy through the sheer size of a ring, which extends the suspended, noble floors of the heart of the preexisting building. The continuity of the public spaces, protected from the elements yet transparent to escaping outward glances, makes the old city and the forests appear far away. (G.C.)

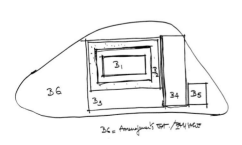

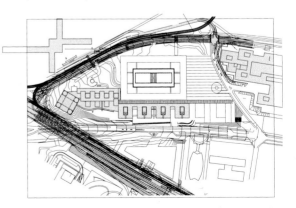

Study-sketch and functional distribution

General floor plan of the complex

The contest model

Detail of the model:
the portico zone with
the spiral stairway

Comprehensive view
of the model with
the lower portico body
and the two towers

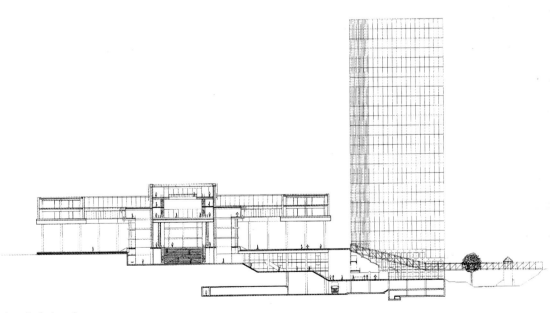

Longitudinal section

Town Hall and Urban Rebuilding
Innsbruck, 1996-2002

In the historic heart of the city of Innsbruck, a complex program was conceived by a heterogeneous client, the city itself along with a group of private investors, with the intention of constructing a new town hall while conserving the antique building. In the spring of 1996, Dominique Perrault was invited to participate in the international competition. Convinced that not only the formal and urbanistic aspects but also the political ones played a fundamental role in the exact comprehension of the project's parameters, Perrault had Rolf Reichert as a partner for this contest project.

Since the competition's first phase, the proposed design promised to be grandiose while simultaneously and completely respecting the location, with the intention of transforming this area of the city into a newly recognizable and modern urban entity, despite its relatively modest dimensions.

Only in January 1998, after the contest's second phase, reduced to Perrault's team along with that of Guido Canali, the jury unanimously decided in favor of the French architect's project, which adequately satisfied the program's formal, functional and urbanistic requests, in addition to the requirements for commercial use.

Recreating a public square-garden, constructing an open building upon this public space, connecting the whole complex with a network of passages and covered galleries, constructing a commercial ground-floor hosting various types of shops, as in a shopping center.

The answer to such a complex program in an historical site in the city's center is based on a construction strategy in interrelated episodes, defining a new skyline for the city. A glass bell-tower emerges above it all, creating a dialectic with the other spires of Innsbruck, but this is not the only dominating element: the town council meeting room is located on the roof-garden, which also provides a restaurant and a generous view of the surrounding mountains. An antique glass court protects a commercial space, similar to a small market, while a tree-lined garden was created in another court. Finally, a large, covered, glass passageway comprises the project's backbone. No less than thirteen artists were involved in the project, among whom Peter Kolger and Daniel Buren, who serigraphed the large glass walls of the common areas with their own works.

As a sedimentation of the traces bearing witness to each epoch, the project gathers and unites various architectural typologies. Glass constitutes the primary material, transparent or white, translucid or enameled. The doors and windows are black, broad or thin depending on whether or not they can be opened. The composition recalls the absolute geometry of Mondrian. Thus, the buildings are partially cloaked in metallic fabric, solar protection or visual protection, which introduce various amounts and types of light —simply, another complexity. This complexity creates a heterogeneous, modern architecture, like the client, like the history of the location and like our European culture, mixing abstraction and representation, commerce and politics, culture and free-time. (G.C.)

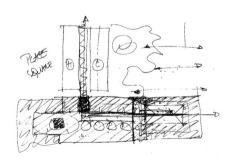

Study-sketch

View of the façade
facing the square

The glass façade with
the commercial gallery

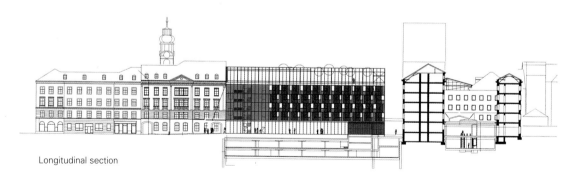

Longitudinal section

General floor plan

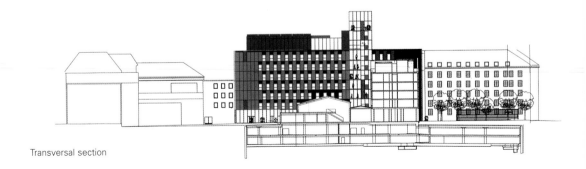

Transversal section

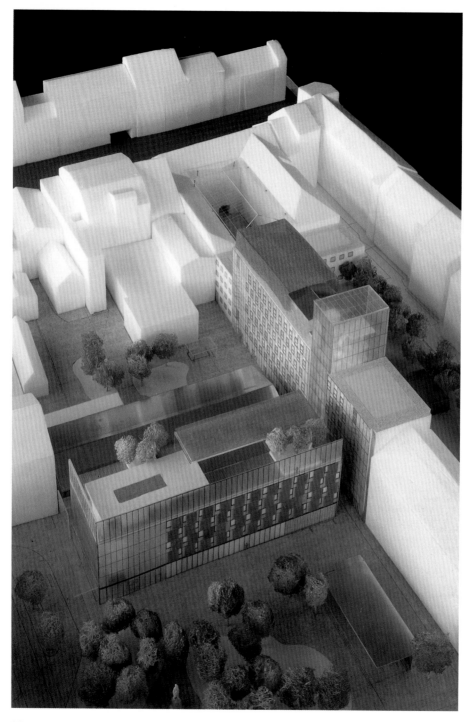

The model

View of the long, checkered
façade opposite the square
of the town hall, with the
central tower in dark glass

Next pages
View of the large, glass
court: the commercial
gallery with the skylight
by Daniel Buren

Southern façade
of the central tower
by Peter Kogler

Media Library
Vénissieux, 1997-2001

The Media Library in Vénissieux is positioned at the intersection of an important, tree-lined urban axis and the north-south artery that flanks the city's town hall, serving as a hub of connection between the historical zone and the habitat's southern development. It functions as "a large house", with a multipurpose yard and other mutable aspects generated by a dichotomy: from the exterior it appears closed, like a building that is protecting itself from the world; from the interior, it is permeated by light, open to the city and to the world. It is a location of cultural alliance, of exchange.

Dominique Perrault constructed a smooth-surfaced, sober-looking glass volume, marked by the structural rhythm of elements in metal, composed of precariously mounted, perforated boxes. This "filling" confers a very particular life and luminosity, as well as a unique identity to the Media Library. Within, all the functions are united on a single level and are surrounded by a peristyle. This space encloses the Media Library's various functions and simultaneously provides a "public" circulation and the acoustic and thermal isolation necessary for the rooms. The size of the path creates a possible exhibition space and an instructive and enjoyable walk: on one side open to the natural ambient and on the other, to the cultural activities that take place there.

The ease of movement on a single level and without hierarchy confers an intimate, almost introspective dimension to this architecture. The mobility and the flexibility of the locations add a dimension of contemporaneity tied to the movement of man and culture.

In the heart of this assemblage is the hall, a sort of urban passage, linking the planned square on the west side with the nature —also specifically designed— which extends to the east on a higher elevation. The offices, located on the top floor of the tower-blade at the center of the Media Library, are reached from the hall. In addition, the roof is perforated with different sized openings that allow light to enter the center of the building during the day.

With respect to their functions, the offices form an independent entity, which is nevertheless connected to the library's activity.

The fixed partitions and the furniture are extremely simple and linear, in homogeneous materials —as the floor continues in exposed cement— with the intention of providing a container, ready to receive other furniture (mobile and non), sliding elements, such as enormous curtains and colored partitions made with a large variety of materials, to define a happy and vivacious environment. The economy of the design resides in its simplicity; the building is constituted by a single floor that contains the Media Library and a small body for offices and services.

The entire construction is treated with "raw" materials: exposed concrete, cement floors, the galvanized steel structure, opaque and transparent glass, guaranteeing a significant conservation of energy partially obtained through the central gallery, which serves as an interspace of passage for the entire system. (G.C.)

Study-sketch

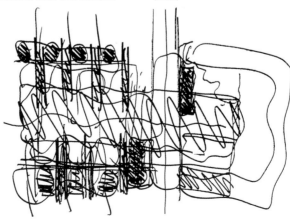

Comprehensive view of the
façade facing the street

Sketch of the distributional
scheme

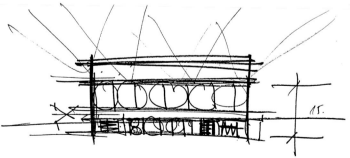

Front elevation and
longitudinal section

Plan

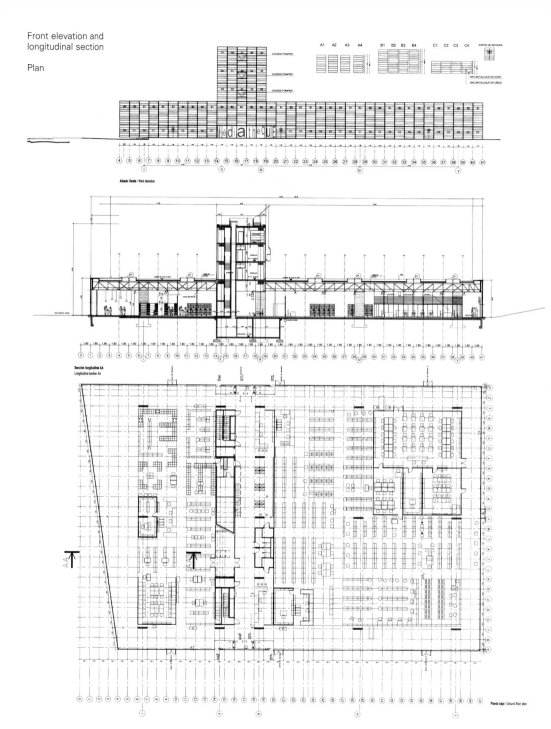

Alzado Oeste / West elevation

Sección longitudinal AA
Longitudinal section AA

Planta baja / Ground floor plan

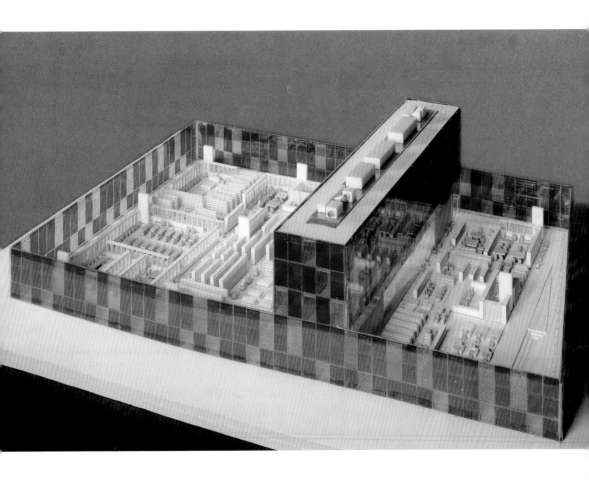

View of the façade with
access to the transversal
gallery

Detail of the façade

Interior view: the large
window facing the street

Interior view: illumination
system of the hall and one
of the reading rooms

Detail of the structural
system in steel and glass

M-Preis Supermarkets
Austria, 1999-2003

In 1999, Dominique Perrault is assigned the realization of the first of a series of new supermarkets for the well-known Austrian chain, M-Preis, in Wattens, Tyrol. In this case, the architect, already famous in Austria as the winner of the contest for the planning of the new Town Hall in Innsbruck, is faced with the task of joining food distribution with design, creating an innovative and modern building. The supermarket comes into being in a mountainous area, situated in proximity to the Swarovski crystal factory, an element which, according to Perrault himself, has served as the principle source of inspiration for the creation of the M-Preis building. In fact, it is developed as a crystal object with a rigorously geometric layout extending on only one level, with a comprehensive area of 1,500 square meters. Realized in only four months, it is constituted by two predominant materials: glass and cement. The glass surfaces, inserted into argentine metal grills, allow the reflection of the alpine landscape; birches and larches constitute the small artificial woods, inserted within a sinuously flowing structure, adjacent to the glass walls. The only completely transparent glass is the one facing the garden, whereas the other faces of the prefabricated structure are constituted by less-than-crystalline glass walls that acquire various gradations depending on the atmospheric conditions. The only cement wall is in the back, where the building ends, delimiting various spaces for offices and storage.

The distribution of interior spaces follows a logic, which is functional to the sale of the products: the open space hosts the outermost shelves on the building's shortest side, whereas the counters and other shelving are located in the central area. The style of the furnishing is rigorously hi-tech, with illumination provided by ceiling-hung track lighting; the ceiling itself is formed of multilayered, wood-colored Osb panels, which purposely contrast the dark-colored floor panels. On the exterior, the main entrance is located under a large, jutting marquise upon which the supermarket's cubic logo is displayed. The overall idea that is conveyed by the completed project is that of a functional and comfortable space, where the prevailing sense of well-being infects the shopper, who is also invited to take advantage of the relaxation areas such as the café and the pastry shop within.

For the second of the M-Preis supermarkets, also located in Wattens, Perrault follows the same common thread that inspired the planning of the first: the use of the same materials and the attention to light, which is once again filtered from the exterior through glass and metal panels. The building is conceived as a transparent space, essential in structure and form, situated above a convenient, underground car park where massive cement pylons delimit the spaces and contribute to the support of the upper level. The entrance is furnished with a ramp and stairs, with a metal handrail, leading to an antecedent space hosting tables and chairs beneath vast umbrellas: a relaxation area for those seeking refreshment at the café. The building not only hosts the space dedicated for food sales, but also a police post and other areas dedicated to shopping. The decision to create these new internal spaces arises from the supermarket's need for multifunctionality, to create a public space as a place for communication and meeting.

The last of the M-Preis supermarkets is constructed on the banks of the Inn River in Zirl; it is completely integrated with the context of the landscape. Its structure is constituted by glass panels, whereas the metal roof assumes the guise of a large platform. The project was realized in six months and once again calls for a café and an external car park. The concept of both interior and exterior space is identical to that of the other supermarkets; even here, before its function as a supermarket, it is a gathering center with a strong communicative value. Over an area of 2,000 m^2, the alternating use of glass and metal, constant in all three projects, becomes a recognizable trait of the commercial trademark. At the same time, the light composition of these materials allows the fusion of architecture and vegetation so that the building is not an isolated object, but rather participates in the context of the landscape. (C.M.)

Wattens I. Comprehensive
view of the front facing
the street with the park
area's curvaceous fence

Wattens I.
View of the model

Study diagram

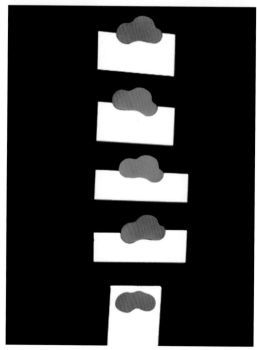

Wattens I. The three
façades: the main façade,
facing the street and
hidden by the park,
the lateral façade, entirely
in glass, and the well-hidden
façade, corresponding
to the warehouses

Wattens I. Detail
of the main entrance

Detail of the system
of glass façades

Detail of the lateral façade

Wattens I. View of the completely transparent interior with the system of illumination and shelving designed by Perrault

Wattens II. General
floor plan of the work

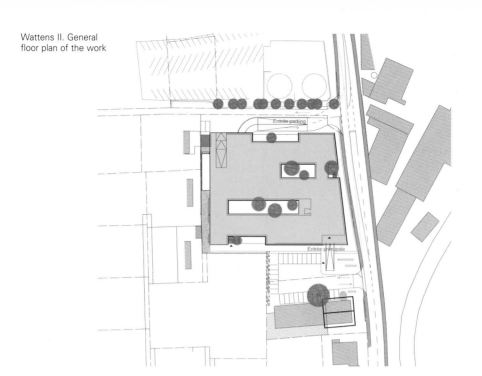

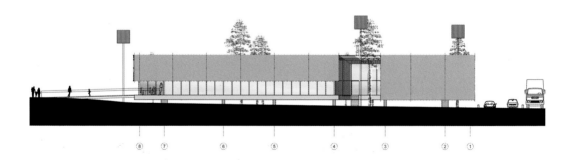

In alto il fronte nord e in
basso il fronte sud.

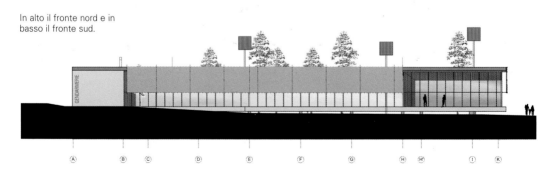

Wattens II. View of the
main entrance and its detail

Wattens II. Entrance
to the car park

View of the parking area
beneath the building

The lateral façade

The façade facing the street

Wattens II. Interior view

Detail of the "hidden" frontal elevation from the street

Zirl. Comprehensive
view of the parking area:
the main entrance to the
supermarket is evidenced
by the covering

Plan

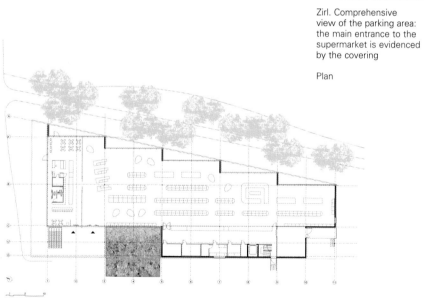

Detail of the inclined glass
in relation to the surrounding
park area

Transversal and longitudinal
section

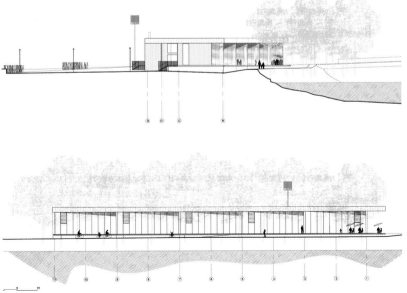

Zirl. Nocturnal view of the
entrance with the illuminated
shelter of the jutting
covering and the inclined
lateral façade

Detail of the relationship
between interior
and exterior: the walls'
transparency creates
a unity between illumination
and nature

Interior view: above,
the cafeteria, below, the
supermarket's shelving

Ewha University Campus Center
Seoul, 2004-2007

Winner of an international competition held in February 2004, the Ewha Campus Center project, exclusively for women, represents a linear crevice that creates a new topography for the area, revealing the campus interior. In this empty space, a heterogeneous form takes place, which permits the hosting of a great variety of activities. A gently sloping boulevard directs circulation while descending to a monumental stairway that leads visitors to the highest point of the campus.

In his own words, Perrault recognizes the Champs-Elysées of Paris and the Campidoglio of Rome as the project's inspirational elements, which simultaneously represents a court of entrance to the various departments, a forum for the exchange of ideas after class, a square, a place for pause and relaxation hosting a café, and last but not least, an open air theatre, comprising the stairway, whose terraced concavity lends itself well to the functions of an amphitheatre.

This real and conceptual flexibility allows the new Ewha Campus to integrate itself with the area as a building, as a landscape and as a sculpture. Along the slit, the campus opens up to pedestrians, welcoming their flowing through the site. These "Champs Elysées" attract the public, leading students and visitors across the area, towards the north, and joining different levels to one another. The pathways between preexisting buildings are conserved, whereas the "bridges", provided in the contest phase, were removed. Subterranean corridors are also in the works to connect the new area with some of the preexisting buildings: a three-dimensional connective system is made possible, thus completing the project's integration with the rest of the campus. The site's complexity is greater when considered in relation to the preexisting elements of the university and to the city of Shinchon to the south. Perrault's proposal is an urban response, a global solution, which interweaves the mesh of the university's site with that of the city surrounding it, enclosing it into a unitary landscape.

With this gesture, the definition of the valley-aperture and the collocation of a section dedicated to athletic activity in the area opposite it, the geography of the location is transformed, undergoing a metamorphosis on various levels. The athletic esplanade, like the valley, assumes various functions, giving the campus a new doorway of accessibility, a platform for athletic activities and a space for festivals and manifestations. This area creates a concrete tie between the university and the city: a public space for everyone, which exhibits university life to the inhabitants of Shinchon.

The bucolic nature of the campus, its most remarkable quality, involves both the exterior as well as the interior. The park becomes an ideal garden, a special place for meeting during breaks between classes, a place of relaxation. Here, the distinction between old and new is blurred, the construction and the landscape, the present and the past. Above and below the park, once occupied by Ewha Square and the athletic field, the new university offers spaces for instruction and student services. The university center must offer a new direction to higher education in the 21st century. It will establish organic relationships between the center and the areas surrounding the university, just as with the areas on the surface and below the ground, and will provide accessibility to the university from the main street of Jung Mun. (G.C.)

Study-sketch

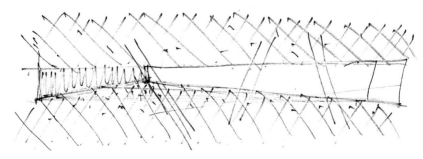

General view of the
campus

General floor plan

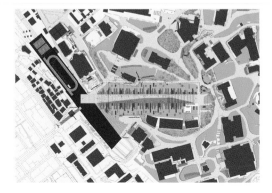

Contest model

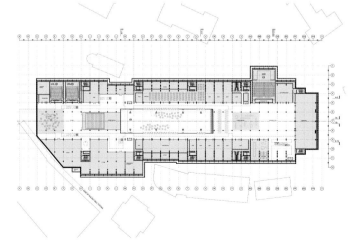

Plan of the college

Rendering of the project:
the sloping boulevard and
the façades of the new
buildings

View of the model with the
study for the park system

The area dedicated
to athletic activity,
the "sport strip"

Comprehensive view
of the project

Rendering of the project:
an innovative college,
a new system of walkways
and a suggestive urban
park for Seoul

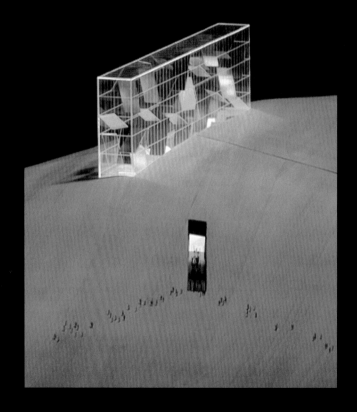

Chapter II

The Season of Contests
*Since the end of the nineties, the primary focus of Dpa has been
on architectural contests as a vehicle for linguistic research.
The importance of the planning process as an instinctive rationality*

Many have questioned the purpose of contests in architecture, even in the
past, and more recently, the methodology of this instrument has been the
focus of numerous debates, above all in Italy, where procedures are not always clear and difficulties tied to the Merloni law[1] have given rise to reflections
and positions of various nature. What more, a public competition quite different from a private one, and a contest among invited contestants is different from an open one, just as a competition in a single phase is not the
same as one comprised of multiple phases, of which at least one is anonymous. But the fact remains that the confrontation in architecture seems to
be at the center of every stimulus, and the occasion of a contest, preferably
an international one, becomes an important moment of exchange and even
cultural interaction. In this sense, the media hype that develops around the
course of the competition, when this is, for example, a particularly significant and relevant one, is also a marvelous cultural conductor which, despite the debates, brings an important flow and exchange of information
on the state of architecture and planning. Perrault, who made his debut in
the "Olympics" of architecture expressly through an important competition,
that of the Bibliothèque nationale, after a period including direct commissions, decided to make the vehicle of contests a priority in his studio's activity. In an interview, he expounded upon the subject: "I came into being
thanks to competitions, not direct commissions, but in the last few years a
problem has arisen which has since become a law: competitions must be
anonymous. Yet behind every project, there is an architect! In this sense,
France would dissent, as we are dealing with an intellectual work and therefore one not separable from the person who produces it. Truly a juridical
question... We would need to redefine the cultural framing of contests,
which fundamentally represent an occasion for the debate of ideas. Actually, we would need more places, open to the public, where plans elabo-
rated in the context of the various competitions could be exposed, so as not
to keep them hidden within the realm of examining boards. In the context
of examining administration and politics, the contest is a detestable instrument that even allows for manipulation. Twenty years ago, France was
very advanced in the politics of high-level cultural and public commissions.
Today the situation is more complex". Fortunately, after such a declaration,
the involvement of DPA in important international competitions has remained
constant. The season of contests in the new millennium had provided two
interesting "tail end" occasions for the 20th century —competitions held
in 1999— on the theme of cultural and artistic locations. It was no coincidence that these were taken on by Perrault with the almost intangible compactness, due to its transparency, of the prismatic extension of the Muse-

um Reina Sofia in Madrid[2] and of the City of Culture in Santiago de Compostela[3] which, in the unity of its gesture, a luminous beacon upon the hill of culture, anticipates the idea of landscape's artificialization, the theme of the optical instrument successively expressed in the Centre Pompidou in Metz as well. In this case, the language of Perrault is not yet focused upon the necessity of covering/uncovering through the use of "metallic veils" that create interstitial spaces, but continues with the idea of transparency and traversability, if even purely visible, of the planned space, as in the Bibliothèque nationale, Kansai Kan and the Media Library. These are based upon a parallelepiped, traversed in its internal sections by inclined reflective panes and truly and completely developed within the hill, in its depth, between highly elevated spaces and environments of the most widely varied dimensions and functions, according to a symmetrically distributed scheme relative to the backbone of the transparent block. "A kaleidoscope that transforms the landscape into architecture and the architecture into landscape"[4]. In the project for Madrid[5], on the other hand, the rust-proof, gold colored, metallic mesh "adorns the museum with a luminous halo and protects it from the ardor of the sun"[6]. A double skin, which runs along the front of the new entranceway-square destined for sculptures, seems to detach itself from its perimeter, inclining as it designs a public space opposite the south side of the existing museum. The reference is evident here to the first luminous prism of the Hotel Belier, which so strongly characterizes the area of the outskirts of Paris between the ring road and the Bibliothèque. The Madrid competition was an extremely interesting occasion, with projects of great significance, concluding with the victory of Nouvel and the taking of second place by Perrault. The former proposed a division of the program into three bodies, reunified by the enormous, "light wing, colored as the roofs [...] of Madrid"[7] in complete respect of the antique, 18th century hospital, conserving its arboreal essence, whereas the latter —just as Mansilla & Tunon, also among the finalists, with a project that presented numerous similarities to that of Perrault, including the collocation on the plot and the relation to the preexisting— chose a parallelepiped building developing in verticality, completely separate from the preexisting; a luminous sheet which, in its confrontation with the building by Sabatini, redesigns the surrounding public and functional space[8]. The theme of the sheet-tower, to be installed into the skyline of the Spanish metropolises, will yet remain in the imagination of Perrault's plans, who, after two hotel commissions, one in Madrid and one in Barcelona[9], is finally creating the second of the regular, yet axially disjointed silhouettes —recalling the contest-project of Gropius and Meyer for the Chicago Tribune[10]— characterized by a surface that is continually perforated by oculi.

Among the more recent opportunities, in addition to the suggestive Theatre Mariinsky, presently in the phase of realization and a discussion of which is exposed in the following interview with the author, the international competition for the new home of the Centre Pompidou in Metz[11] must be mentioned. In 2003, the well known Parisian cultural institution decides to decentralize and to create an appendix in Metz, calling a competition among 157 invited candidates, of whom six finalists —Stéphan

Perrault's proposal for the contest for the extension of the Museo Reina Sofia in Madrid

Maupin-Pascal Cribier, Herzog & de Meuron, Foreign Office Architects, Nox, Dominique Perrault and Shigeru Ban Architects— with the conclusive victory of the team led by Ban, which included Jean De Gastines and Philip Gumuchdajian. The winning project presents, among other things, conceptual analogies to the more recent research of Perrault. In fact, the victorious group opts for a fragmentary intervention in episodes, by no means the cubes proposed by the French architect, but three differently oriented parallelepiped telescopes, positioned upon high *pilotis* and unified by means of a wood and metal manta composed of hexagonal elements and covered by a membrane of translucid fiber. In actuality, this proposal clearly recalls, even more than the project proposed for this very contest, which was similarly enveloped in a vibrant mantle, Perrault's plans for the Mariinsky Theatre, where the fragmentation of the parts determines the definition of a series of intermediate public spaces, utilizable independently from the theatre's principle activity which, in the case of Saint Petersburg, is dedicated to opera; even more so, it resembles his proposal for the home of the new Pinault Foundation.

In the case of Metz, Dpa proposes a new interplay of full and empty cubes, perfectly aligned to define a single parallelepiped body located beneath a metallic tent. An elementary prism enclosed by a thin covering of shining silver, like a mirror which, as an optical "instrument", creates effects of diffraction and movement. A "movement" anticipated by the idea of nomadism, which is implied by the very image of the tent. A structure in woven steel mesh, anchored to the ground through guys that alter its profile, making it almost a "catenary". As the designer himself stated in an essay, "it was not about thinking of a small nor of a large Beaubourg…"[12].

In accordance with his research on coverings begun in conjunction with the construction of the Olympic velodrome and pool in Berlin, later becoming the enveloping covering in the contest-project for the Pinault Foun-

The large, golden shell of the Mariinsky opera house in Saint Petersburg

Project for the contest for the Centre Pompidou in Metz

dation (2001) and the much-decorated Mariinsky Theatre (2003), Perrault returns to the theme of metallic mesh coverings here in Luxembourg, a gesture which tends to amplify and control the characteristics of luminosity and climate of the buildings themselves, as well as of those environments which are neither interior nor exterior. One could certainly not consider Metz as a return to the primitive hut[13], the Laugierian and trilithic concept is quite distant; it is, however, a Froebelian effect which uses the impalpable enveloping element to assume a media value, self-representative, transforming the "tent" into a screen for the cultural center. The heart of the museum, on the other hand, is the great, high nave, around which are positioned the exhibition rooms, some of which face the city, offering a special perspective of the panorama. But it is in the plan for the Ile Seguin in Boulogne Billancourt, destined to the Foundation of Contemporary Art on commission by the collector François Pinault —a contest by invitation for what was formally the Renault industrial area, won by Tadao Ando, who, in the final phase, beat Perrault along with other significant protagonists of the international panorama, including Manuelle Gautrand, Steven Holl, Rem Koolhaas and MVRDV— that this theme reaches an even higher level of expression, such that it was presented by its designer as "a gift", or rather, a gift bag. A pale ghost upon the island occupied by part of the area. A proposal of strong urban connotation, with the public spaces planned as an integral part of the composition through absolutely linear and variously directed geometrical volumes, which resemble the silhouette of an enormous sail in the wind; but this time it is not a tent that stretches out without ever touching the structure below it, but rather a sheet of metallic mesh which, gently affixed to the volumes below, outlines their forms and accents the suggestivity. Perrault's involvement on the Parisian island does not terminate with the results of this contest; a few years later, in 2004, Dpa chooses to participate in the competition for the restructuring of the landscape on the Ile Seguin, alongside the world-famous artist Daniel Buren, with whom he has maintained a close collaboration for some time[14].

Fondation Pinault
in Boulogne Billancourt:
study-model

[1] Law 109/94 (L.11 February 1994, n.109), outline law regarding public works.

[2] Contest won by Jean Nouvel with the only proposal that divided the program into three bodies with respect to the historical preexistence of the area. Second place for Perrault.

[3] Contest won by Peter Eisenman. The City of Culture of Galicia consists of a complex ensemble of six buildings occupying an area of 212,000 m². The project, winner of the International Competition held in 1999 by the Department of Culture, Social Communications and Tourism of the City Council of Galicia, is currently under construction.

[4] Translation by D. Perrault, *Relation to the contest-project*, a text which calls for a precise declaration of intent: "Nous avons incrusté un grand instrument optique dans la colline pour transformer la géographie en architecture".

[5] 'Contest for the extension of the Centro de Arte Reina Sofia', *Casabella*, 682, October 2000, p. 8.

[6] D. Perrault, 'Relation to the contest-project for the exension of the Centro de Arte Reina Sofia', *Casabella*, 682, October 2000, p. 13.

[7] J. Nouvel, 'Relation to the contest-project for the exension of the Centro de Arte Reina Sofia', *Casabella*, 682, October 2000, p. 11.

[8] In contrast, both Cruz & Ortiz as well as Nouvel decided upon an organization around a courtyard, whereas compact blocks characterize the proposals of Navarro Baldeweg and Vazquez Consuegra, opposing in the typological organization of the fragmentation of the irregular forms chosen by Zaha Hadid and Eric Miralles.

[9] The project was also presented at the 8th Architecture Biennial in Venice, "Next", curated by Deyan Sudijc, in the "towers" section.

[10] Walter Gropius and Adolf Meyer, 1922.

[11] *Concours Centre Pompidou – Metz*, Édition du Moniteur et Édition du Centre Pompidou, Paris, 2004.

[12] D. Perrault, *Le Musee et la Ville: une tente*, in *Concours Centre Pompidou – Metz*, Édition du Moniteur et Édition du Centre Pompidou, Paris, 2004, p. 122.

[13] M.A. Laugier, cit.

[14] Cf. note 12, p. 19.

Centre Pompidou in Metz: rendering of the interior

City of Culture of Galicia
Santiago de Compostela, 1999

This project is presented for the international contest held by the Department of Culture, Social Communications and Tourism of the City Council of Galicia for the realization of a new cultural pole in the area of Mt. Gaias, intended to be transformed into a new "destination of pilgrimage".

The relief of the area, located downstream from the dense vegetation of the Woods of Galicia, is completely nude and in contrast to the dense and compact urban fabric of the historical center in close proximity.

Upon its summit is positioned a transparent covering, a prism of glass characterized by extreme formal clarity and a stereometric compactness that transform it into a strongly distinctive sign and catalyst. The intervention on the landscape is punctual, but buries its roots in a much deeper ground; in fact, the visible architecture represents merely the "tip of the iceberg" of a primarily hypogeal project that is developed over nine floors of hollow spaces, created by subtraction and leaving no indication of their presence on the surface, other than a cleft along the slope, which provides an emergency exit. The principle functions hosted, Library, Museum, Theatre and Auditorium, are developed to various heights, in dimensionally different spaces and are organized symmetrically relative to the longitudinal glass artery that flowers on the surface.

This body is conceived and utilized as a true "optical instrument", a "laboratory object"*, capable of capturing light and transporting it into the various hidden spaces through a sophisticated mechanism of strategically aimed and positioned mirrors and shades in its interior, which serve to reflect not only light, but also images. In this way, the project interprets the relationship between interior and exterior in a stimulating way. "from the interior, we can see the external landscape and some fragments of the city of Santiago de Compostela; from the exterior, we can see inside the construction's body, as if through an endoscope"*.

The transparencies and the structural lightness dematerialize the volumetric impact of this object, which interferes so little with the surrounding landscape, and rather, like a "kaleidoscope", succeeds in blurring the boundaries between nature and architecture. The same concept characterizes the idea of the winning plans of Peter Eisenman, nevertheless designed according to a plastic and dynamic language which, evoking the figure of a shell, symbol of the city, "manipulates" the terrain, cutting it, lifting it and corrugating it. (G.G.)

* Translation by D. Perrault, *Relation to the contest-project.*

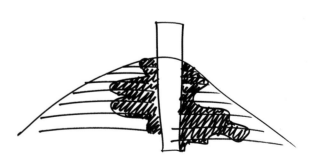

Study-sketches: the lantern by day and by night

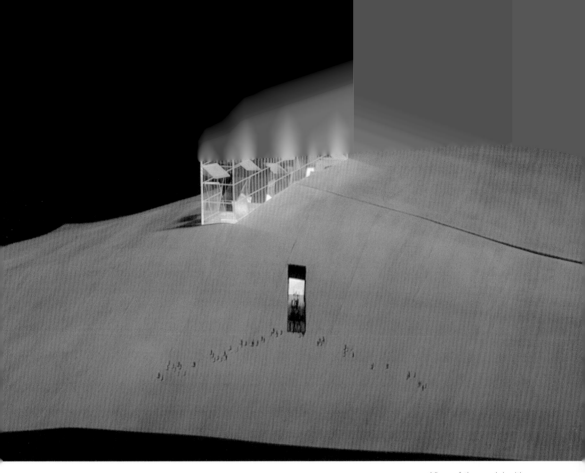

View of the model with
the crystalline prism

Insertion into the territorial
context

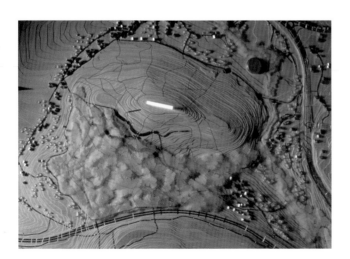

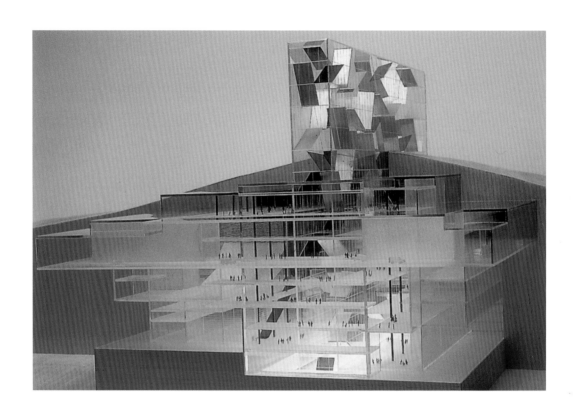

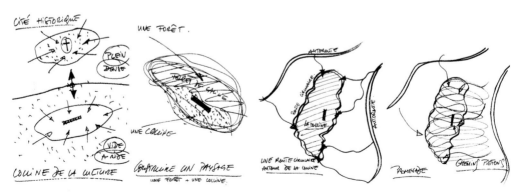

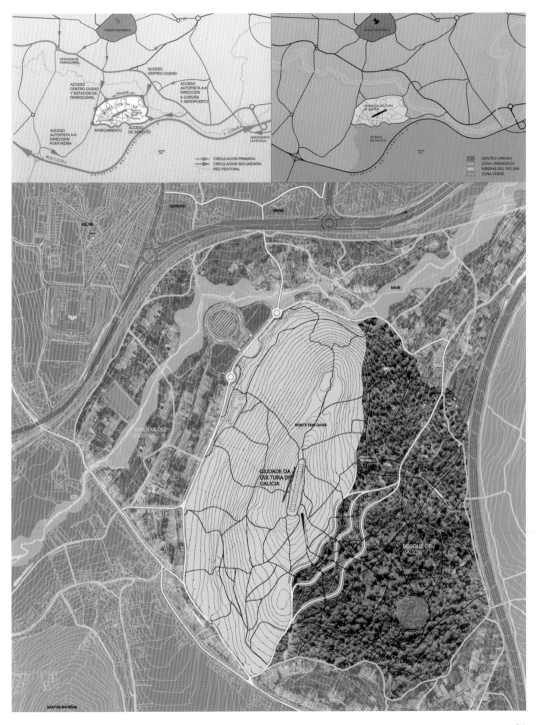

Diagrams and distributive
sections of the project

Rendering of the interior
space, partially to full
height and to the balconies

Detail of the comprehensive
model

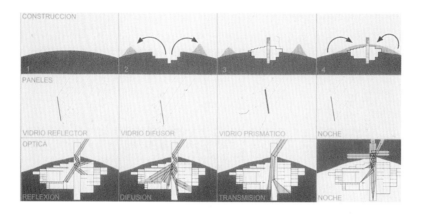

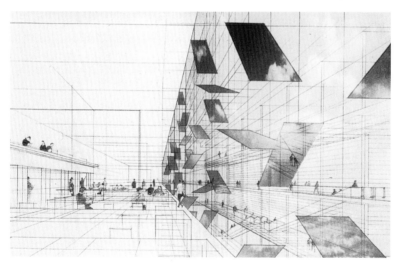

Extension of the Reina Sofia Museum
Madrid, 1999

At the beginning of the eighties, the 18th century complex of the antique General Hospital of Madrid served as an appropriate home for the Museo Nacional Centro de Arte Reina Sofia. Now, however, the need for renovated and larger spaces tied to culture and art has given rise to the consideration of an operation of expansion, translated in 1999 into an international competition. In the panorama of competing projects, the winning proposal by J. Nouvel was the most respectful of the Sabatini building, characterized by its partitioning into three bodies, recomposed beneath a sort of protective wing.

Dominique Perrault's project, taking second place, is inspired by an opposing concept which, utilizing less than one third of the available trapezoidal area, is configured in a single, compact, vertical volume, isolated and in clear contrast to its context.

In fact, it is a golden prism that "faces", with over eight floors, the southern view of the historic edifice, giving the urban fabric a new public space: a square, also part of an artistic circuit with open-air sculpture exhibitions.

The only direct link with the museum and its extension is comprised of a new nucleus of passages which, positioned next to the original center, joins four floors of the existing building with those of the new.

On the ground floor is the main entrance, to the south-east, and a reception vestibule housing the cafeteria, the bookstore and access to the exhibition halls and to the sublevel, where the auditorium and meeting rooms are located, surrounded by a flexible space for hosting various events. This area, constituting an independently functioning machine, is intended for use even when the center itself is closed, providing a new concept of the museum as an open space for contemporary society.

The rear, on the other hand, is occupied by a functional access and service area for employees and is further distinguished through the material treatment of its façade. The transparent glass shell enclosing the entire building is covered by a precious, gold-colored fabric along the side of the main entrance, on the Ronda de Atocha.

Like a scenic curtain, this is inclined towards the square, beneath the covering's jutting wing (which protects visitors on the panoramic terrace) and extends the public space to its interior. Depending on the visual perspective, this metallic mesh assumes diaphanous effects and varying degrees of permeability, a sort of osmotic film that serves as a filter between the museum and the city, inviting visitors to discover its true identity. (G.G.)

Detail of the contest model

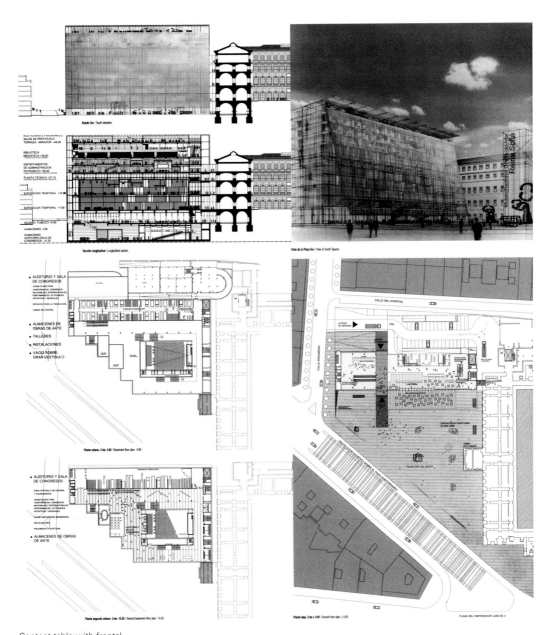

Contest table with frontal
elevations, sections, plans
and general floor plan

View of the contest model:
the transparency of the
secondary façade and the
double skin, barely lifted
away, allowing access
to the "new" square

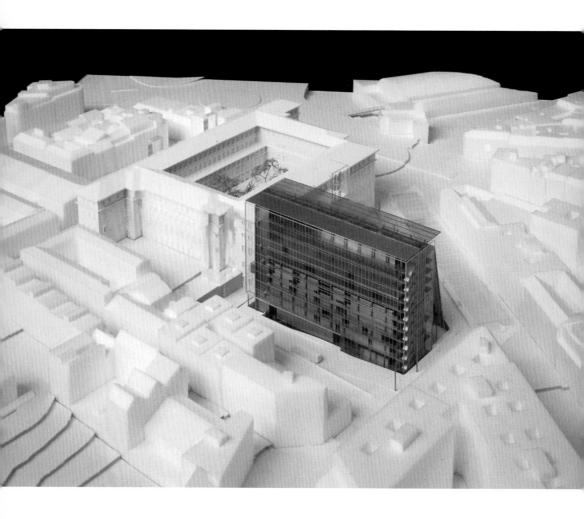

Fondation François Pinault
Ile Seguin, Boulogne-Billancourt, 2001

The Center for Contemporary Art desired by the François Pinault Foundation would have been constructed upon the Island of Seguin in Boulogne-Billancourt near Paris, in the former Renault industrial area, if the owner had not recently changed intentions, orienting himself towards the collocation of his collection in Palazzo Grassi in Venice.

The planner of the center, which will no longer be created, is Tadao Ando, who participated in the 2001 international competition by invitation, beating in the final phase Manuelle Gautrand, Steven Holl, Rem Koolhaas, MVRDV, Alvaro Siza and Dominique Perrault.

With the hopes of offering a "pendant" to the Guggenheim Museum of Bilbao, the foundation would have occupied an area of 3.2 hectares, with a construction of 32,000 square meters and a sculpture garden. In addition, it would have been connected to the ground by two new ramps: a 14 meter wide bridge with a light of 100 meters (for which another contest was held) and a catwalk.

Dominique Perrault's proposal for this art center is defined by the author himself as "a gift" that would transfigure the collection and the location. The theme of transfiguration, at the root of the project, requires a process in seven acts, which in turn implies the notion of disintegration.

The first act, the foundational one, defines the transformation of the location's geography, with the integration of a base-platform that occupies the entire surface, installing a new horizontality and a new concept of ground-level on the island.

The second act elevates this area to one of urbanity through the realization of a sequence of minerals and vegetation along the paths and the walkway.

The third act, which offers a single, precious access for everyone from the Seine, is the ramp: conducting to the river, it becomes a meeting point and entranceway to the Foundation.

The narthex, the fourth act, is a flexible structure, stretching between the building and the platform, which provides breathing room between container and exterior while amplifying the desire to "offer and open".

Fifth act: the attention given to the visitors, who have access to the four buildings, through "breathing spaces", which allow them to freely choose their own itinerary.

Sixth act: the multiplicity of possibilities. The galleries unfold on the same floor in a variety of forms, allowing the exhibition of all possible types of works.

Finally, the seventh and final act is the experience itself: a series of white volumes gives each activity its own autonomy, establishing an intimacy in the visitor's meeting with art.

The François Pinault Foundation gives life to a panorama enshrouded in mystery. The minimalist gesture of connecting the volumes that constitute the building with the ample platform determines a radically new volume, which flows directly from the creative process. The "process" generates the architectural form that is in turn obtained by stretching rolls of metallic fabric over the Pinault Foundation, over the extension of the Mariinsky Theatre in Saint Petersburg, over the Olympic Tennis Center in Madrid, becoming a leitmotiv for Perrault. "It all began with the National Library of France", explains the architect, "I needed a covering material that was both manageable and fireproof. I thought about fiberglass, but I finally decided on the metallic mesh."

This metallic mesh, which has invaded his constructions and shortly thereafter, those of a fair number of other architects, "from a decorative element, has become an autonomous structure from which wires can be hung for the connection of electricity". Materials evolve, as do forms and colors. Golden in the bronze version, argentine in the steel version, flattened or draped according to the tension of the cables, the mesh provokes all inspirations. "We have to consider buildings as bodies and clothe them. This fabric is a little pullover, an overall, a scarf, a pashmina...". For the Island of Seguin, it is precisely a net that captures buildings, as in a fish trap. From this metal, Perrault can generate coverings that seem to be made of silk, playing between apparition and disappearance, between presence and absence, with surprising mastery.

Ideal for filtering light and offering a dimmed lighting. "I love the sensuality of this material, its ductility", says Perrault. "It softens the architecture, makes it less definitive. In fact, opaque from the exterior, the metal fibers are lost in an optical effect from the interior, offering a near-transparency. Like a mysterious and delicate veil." (G.C.)

The contest model: the new Foundation inserted into the urban context and a detail thereof

Study-models:
the foundation's skeleton
wrapped in the skin
of the metallic mesh

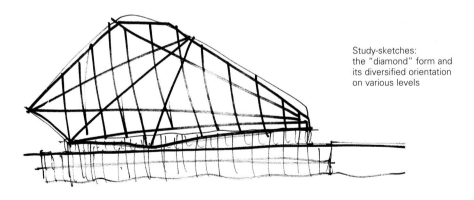

Study-sketches:
the "diamond" form and
its diversified orientation
on various levels

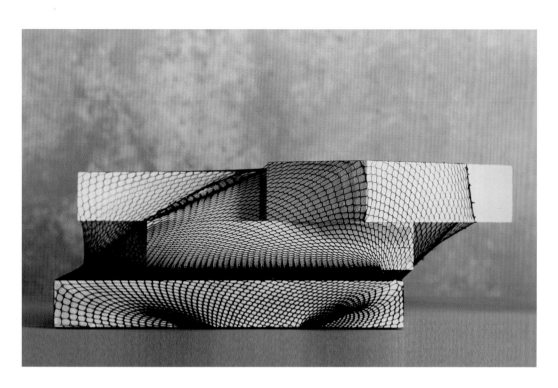

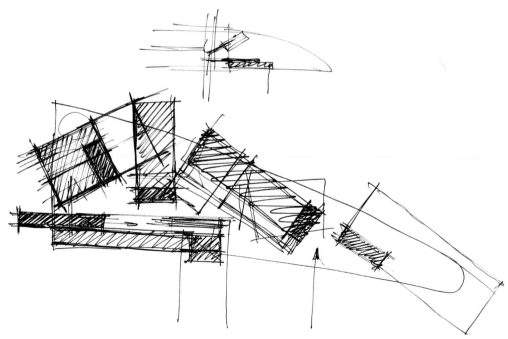

Perspective with the
renovation of the public
spaces

The model

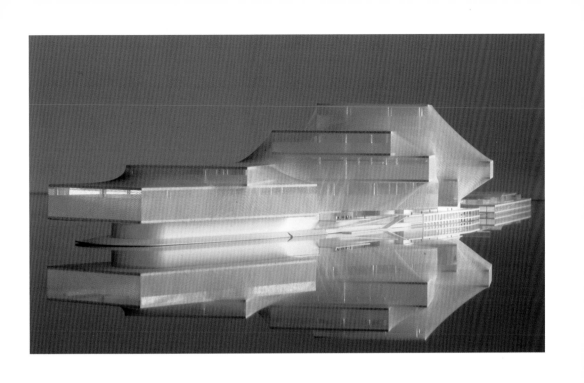

View of the façade facing
the river: the new wharf
and the dynamic and
transparent form of the
Foundation's spaces

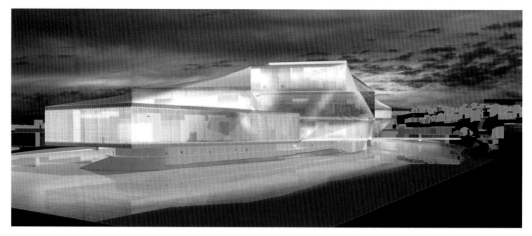

A nocturnal view
and the form by day

Relationship between
interior and exterior:
the city seen from
the cafeteria

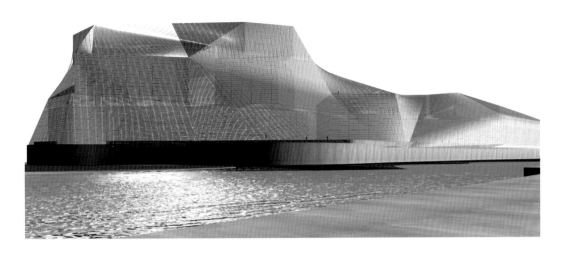

Landscape Renovation of the Ile Seguin with Daniel Buren
Boulogne-Billancourt, 2004

This project for the realization of a "façade-container" for the Ile Seguin (180,000 m²) was undertaken by Perrault in collaboration with Daniel Buren, one of the most significant artists of the contemporary French panorama. The project foresaw the construction of a perimetric structure positioned behind the basement of the island, with the purpose of embanking the effect of fractioning caused by the new edifications and evidencing the continuity of the islands external profile.

A strong dichotomy characterizes the project proposal, the northern façade being defined as "tactile", the southern as "visual"; it is precisely the texture of the perimetric structure which lends a roughness, allowing one's view to penetrate it at various points along this functional renovation of the island's riverfront.

Perrault moved on to the contest's second phase together with Maupin, Michelin and Tschumi. Members of the jury included Jean Nouvel and Tadao Ando, the latter having already won the contest for the center of contemporary art of the Fondation François Pinault on the same island, a project destined never to leave the blueprints due to Pinault's acquisition of Palazzo Grassi in Venice as the Fondation's new home. (G.C.)

Comprehensive view
of the contest proposal

Detail of the "tactile"
northern façade

The "visual" southern
façade

Detail of the façades'
system of "mesh" screens

Study-sketches by Daniel
Buren

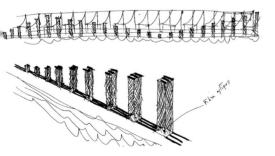

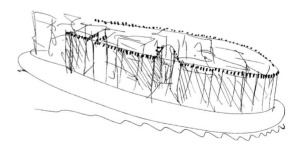

Next pages:
The "tactile" northern
façade

Centre Georges Pompidou
Metz, 2003

Approximately thirty years after its foundation, the Centre Pompidou decides to create its first decentralized appendix in Metz, Lorraine, a strategic position because of its proximity to Germany, Luxembourg and Belgium, capable of internationally promoting the French artistic patrimony of the Parisian exhibition center, in addition to strengthening its own role as a European metropolis.

The project, object of the contest, will take place in the newly formed northern neighborhood of "Amphithéâtre", redesigning a section of the city on the site of an ex-railway station. Taking fourth place, Perrault's studio presents, in the author's own words, a silver-metallic "tent" which, lifting itself from the four sides and opening up at the corners, covers the museum's compact volume. With Shigeru Ban's team (first place), he shares the concept of spatial organization, which creates an intermediate, ambiguously defined place. "This space is identified as being external to the actual museum, yet within the system of visitation and entertainment, and is therefore covered and confined."

Dpa's proposal, nevertheless, identifies itself with "a nomadic architecture", in a structure of temporary character and a completely autonomous configuration that touches the construction beneath it, enlarging its borders, rotating their position and inclining them in elevation, creating various distances between the building and the covering. The stainless steel mesh appears as a recurring stylistic feature in his works, an expression of a process of accurate research and, in Metz, it also becomes a vehicle of communication, animated with visual scenography projected on its surface. Mutating effects of diffraction and reflection, as if generated by an optical device, giving vibrancy to the "peripheral public space", involving the museum's interior and its facades alike. These are primarily treated with an argentine, reflective mirrorization, except for on the ground floor, which features transparent windows.

The volumetric synthesis that governs the structure's exterior is fragmented and decomposed in the interior by means of an interplay of skillfully interlocked volumes and spatial effects modulated to varying heights. Entering through the main entrance, positioned at the south-west, the vast reception area of the forum is accessed, which occupies the two sides of the perimeter, housing the library, the cafeteria and the vertical links. The space is invaded by the jutting volumes of the two upper floors, intended for conferences and administration. Nevertheless, the heart of museum is represented by the great central hall, half of which extends to the museum's full height, destined to host the works of larger dimensions and around which the exhibition rooms of the upper floors are positioned. These, planned according to various dimensional modules, can be visited through an internal walkway that connects them or through a gallery that surrounds them, offering select views of the city. (G.G.)

Study-sketche

General floor plan

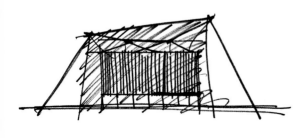

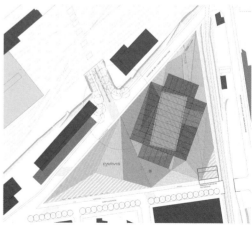

The large "projected" tent
of the new cultural center

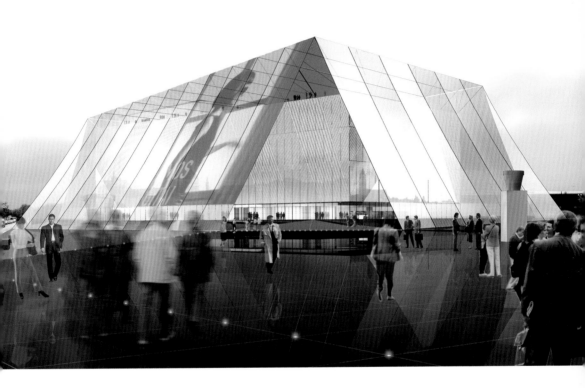

Structural diagram
and functional distribution

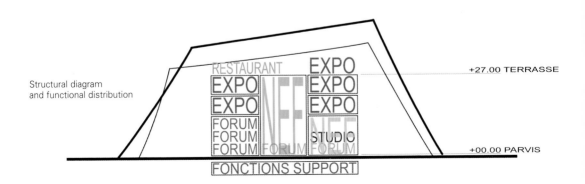

RESTAURANT · EXPO
EXPO · NEE · EXPO
EXPO · · EXPO
FORUM
FORUM · · STUDIO
FORUM · FORUM · FORUM

+27.00 TERRASSE

+00.00 PARVIS

FONCTIONS SUPPORT

The interior exhibition spaces The relationship between
interior and exterior: the
restaurant to the covering,
wrapped by the metallic
mesh

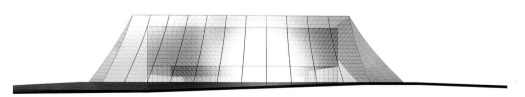

The side elevation

Interior view with the
entrance hall, bookstore,
café, coat room.
On the outside, a work
by Buren

View of the Centre
Pompidou with metallic
mesh structure defining
a series of public spaces
suspended between interior
and exterior, almost
as covered squares

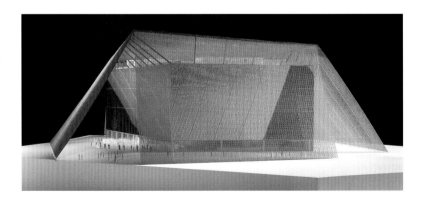

NEF >>>

LIBRAIRIE

VESTIAIRE

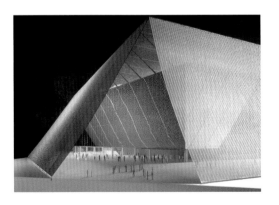

New Mariinsky Theatre
Saint Petersburg, 2003-2009

The extension of the Mariinsky Theatre, in the most recent of Perrault's productions, is one of the most important occasions on an international level. Credit for the initiative is due to the artistic director of the theatre, Valerij Gergiev, who, to no avail advanced the proposal for a new construction in 1997.

It was only in 2003 that an international contest by invitation was called, extended to six international architects —among whom Mario Botta, Arata Isozaki, Hans Hollein, Eric Owen Moss and Erick Van Egeerat— and five Russians, judged by thirteen examiners. For the project's realization, the state provided the considerable financing of one hundred million dollars.

The winner, Perrault, is faced with the task of creating a building of 65,000 square meters, housing a theatre with an auditorium of 2,000 seats, the scenic space and various service areas intended for public use. Among the numerous factors that contributed to the victory to the French architect, one was certainly the attention that he gave to the architectural identity of the city and of the location —with its specificity determined by the proximity of the river— respecting the characteristics and configurations due to climatic variations as well as the noteworthy preexistence surrounding the historic theatre.

The extension is composed of a building comprised of various "stratified" elements; moving outwards from the interior, there is: the opera hall, with its technical machinery, where red and gold projections blend, creating an almost oneiric, strongly scenic atmosphere. The large hall can host 130 musicians, and the audience area is distributed among the orchestra and various levels of balconies. In this environment one clearly perceives a sort of optical illusionism, similar to the tromp l'œil style, which Perrault seems intent on evoking in the decoration of the ceiling, the balconies and the walls of the large hall. Outside, an imposing volume of black marble: the public space, dedicated to restaurants, cafés, shops and other services. The distance between the external covering and this central nucleus allows the upper floors of the building to transform themselves into terraces and balconies at various heights, publicly accessible during the day and at the night, independently from the activities of the theatre.

Through this choice in planning, Perrault was successful in his intention of giving the city "another" place from the building itself, continuing in his research of balance between "private" space and public space. This central nucleus, which houses all of the functions of the theatre, is enclosed in a glass membrane that provides a splendid view of the city from its interior. The external covering is certainly the work's most spectacular element: an enormous golden shell chosen by the architect because it is "the symbol of all Russian monuments". Its asymmetrical structure in gold-colored, anodized aluminum does not follow the building's forms, yet envelops it without touching it, bending around the canal, liberating vast volumes comparable to the underside of a cupola. Its presence does not diminish the preexisting 19th century building, but rather gives it a new significance, connected by a telescopic pathway leading from the golden shell to the historical façade of the Mariinsky. The bridge over the Krykov is completely transparent so as not to oppose the view of the nearby church of Saint Nicolas or clash with the canal's landscape. Perrault's plan gives the theatre a new identity, where the gold, the transparency of glass, the red and the black become the colors that characterize what may become one of the most significant symbols of contemporary Russian architecture. (C.M.)

Study-sketches

The new theater's great golden shell

General floor plan of the project with the new and old theater

View of the contest model

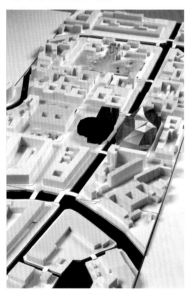

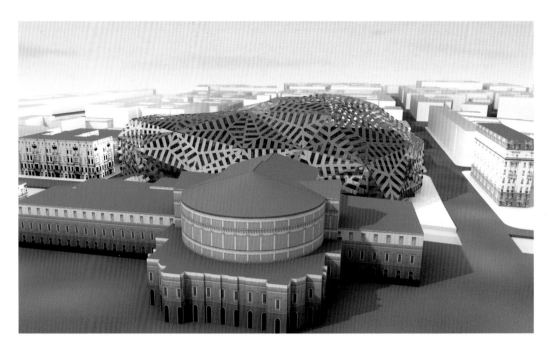

View of the rendering

Comprehensive view of the
project and its insertion in the
urban context

One of the theater's
"long" front elevations

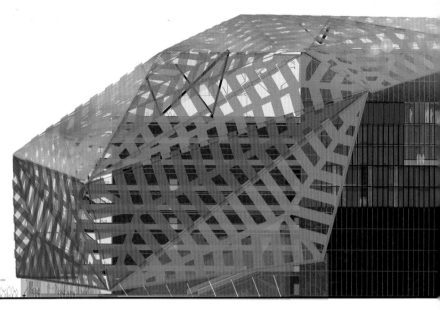

Interior view with the hall
(entire height), characterized
by the suggestive
effect of light provided
by the metallic texture
of the external shell

Study-model
for the diamond form
of the golden cupola

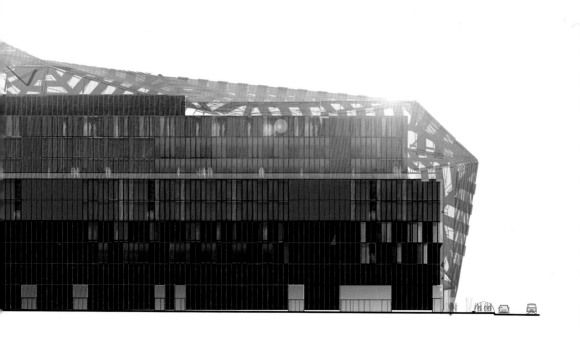

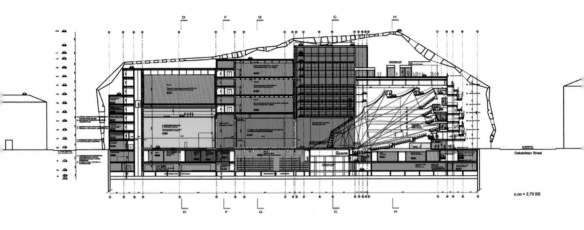

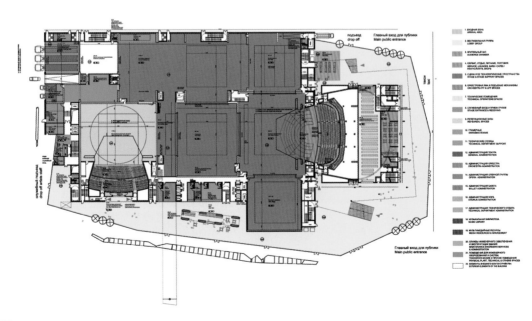

View and section of the
hall: the booths, the stalls,
the stage

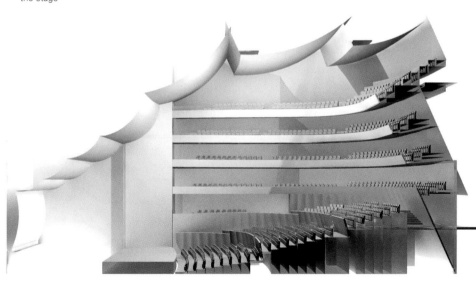

МАРИИНСКИЙ ТЕАТР

№ 4-5   2003

МАРИИНСКИЙ-II ДОМИНИКА ПЕРРО

From a Conversation with Dominique Perrault[1]

One hundred million dollars out of the state's pocket and the new Mariinsky in the New Holland section of Saint Petersburg is about to become a reality. In the former area of the Lithuanian Market, an almost completely destroyed structure of the great 18th century architect, Giacomo Quarenghi, next to the old 19th century Opera, the new theatre of this great Russian city will be erected —precisely in this, the year of its tercentennial celebration. The results of the contest by invitation held in January 2003 by the Russian Federation Government and by the State Academic Mariinsky Theatre for the extension of the historic theatre with a new 2,000-seat auditorium for a utilizable area of 39,000 m² will be determined in May of this year. Joining Russian intellectuals and bureaucrats on the jury, the Italian architect Massimiliano Fuksas seemed explicitly in favor of the project by Hans Hollein, which was beaten two votes to ten by the project of Dominique Perrault. In addition to the winner and the Austrian master, four other architects from the international panorama were invited —Arata Isozaki, Eric Owen Moss, Erick van Egeraat, Mario Botta— along with six Russian planners, Aleksandr Skokan, Andrey Bokov, Oleg Romanov, Andrey Sharov, Sergey Kiselev and Jury Zemtsov.
We are in the suggestive Parisian studio of Dominique Perrault, in the great glass box of the Hôtel Industriel Berlier, his multi-awarded creation from the eighties, which holds a never-ending visual dialogue with the city and with the Library of France. On the seventh floor: the essential office and the architect, plastics and windows. A quick conversation on the recent results of the contest for the Mariinsky Theatre.

The theme of the theatre is an interesting one; I don't believe this type of architecture has yet been confronted. Do you consider this victory in Saint Petersburg a great satisfaction? It is an important international project.
I must say, it is an unexpected victory —a nice surprise.

Really? And yet yours was evidently a strong proposal, "favored" from the very beginning...
Well, I don't know. When I plan, I do it for the moment —not for the past or for the future. I have an emotional relationship with planning, even for contests. I follow an attitude of the moment just as occurs in contemporary art; it is something of an archaic approach, which allows me to shape the context in which I find myself to intervene as if it were a material, a process that allows me any imaginable change of scale.

In effect, the scale of the Mariinsky is an urban one, regarding both the project's remarkable significance as well as the relationship to its context: the preexistences, the canal which separates and joins the two theatres...

As for the Opera theatre, it is possible to speak of two fundamental concepts at the basis of the project.

The first, to make it completely visible on the city's skyline as an important presence for culture itself. The presence of the old 19th century Opera was not particularly evident; thus it was necessary to construct a new one nearby. This idea of the client's was very intelligent, a strong idea. In Paris, for example, moving the new Opera to an entirely different *arondissement* from the Garnier caused a loss of meaning. So, to accentuate this choice, I inserted a building into a complex skyline of cupolas, towers and minarets, giving it a strong gold color, like a new sign, a form that envelops a strongly characterized location.

The second concept is that the Opera is by definition a boring place and not as social as it may seem: in effect, it is only accessible to those possessing a ticket, without which you are completely excluded. With this operation, I want to introduce a social aspect, transparent and not closed, as is usually the case even in contemporary theatres. In the plans for the Mariinsky, the actual Opera is regular and limited —delineated— but the surroundings are open, just as the roof is accessible, providing its most external volume, a panoramic outlook over the city. I feel that this is a positive aspect for a cold and dark city such as Saint Petersburg, where the theatre becomes a beacon, a "golden cocoon", with cafés, restaurants, meeting points, shops and then... also a theatre. For this project, in a certain sense, I resumed the concept of a gallery, of a *passage*: you can traverse it from north to south, and the adjacent canal is a mirror. An asymmetrical golden shell near the canal, where it is reflected in summer; in winter, the frozen canal connects it to its surroundings.

Is it appropriate to think of a reference to 19th century mega-structures such as the Crystal Palace, emblem of the bourgeois and its sociality?

The Crystal Palace was empty, whereas this is a living building; its interior resembles that of a human body, with its flow and continual rapport between internal and external. This plan is the result of a new concept of architectural space, which is unique to this epoch. It is not only about a building or a public space; it is a space connected to its surroundings, and in this sense, my contest-project for the Pinault Foundation (a contest won by Tadao Ando) remains emblematic of this concept.

Therefore, after the "delusion" with the results of the Pinault Foundation, the Mariinsky victory certainly represents an important milestone for your ideological and theoretical plans.

The opportunity in Saint Petersburg was to be able to propose my ideology, my ethics on the theme of public buildings: the idea, that is, to be able to give more than just the building. In my work, there is always a research on the balance between specific space and public space. This opportunity was very interesting for me, because it did not involve an avenue or a piazza; the problem of limit attracts me, and it does not suffice for me that the building is transparent and democratic, but it must be possible to traverse it, to insinuate oneself into it, continually changing the rapport between the interior and the exterior. If you compare, for example, this proposal of mine with some of Frank Gehry's projects, it is natural to think that the initial approach may be similar, but Gehry has a narrative way of transforming form; despite our using the same components and computerized instruments, we obtain different results: his project is a more abstract emptiness, more geometric, Bukminster Fuller-like, politically democratic but more figurative; in his case, this is a purely architectural proposal. For me, form is the final result of a possible transfiguration of a context.

But this form is given in part through certain structures and certain special materials of the latest generation. In this case, an enveloping grating of variable geometry, completely in gold... what is the role of material in your planning concept and, in particular, the role of the metallic mesh ideated for the Mariinsky?
Material is important for light and for flexibility, but it is never the first element I take into consideration. In this case, it will be light and poetic, capable of conferring a new sensation to the ensemble because it is, at the same time, a true structural material, as strong as reinforced cement — never decorative. But it could also be that, in which case it becomes a cloth.

[1] M.V. Capitanucci, 'Il drappo all'Opera', in *Il Nuovo Cantiere*, 2, February 2004.

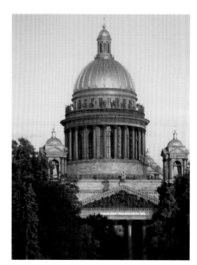

The golden cupolas
of Saint Petersburg

Sketch for the renovation
of the area of the Temple
of Mitra in Naples

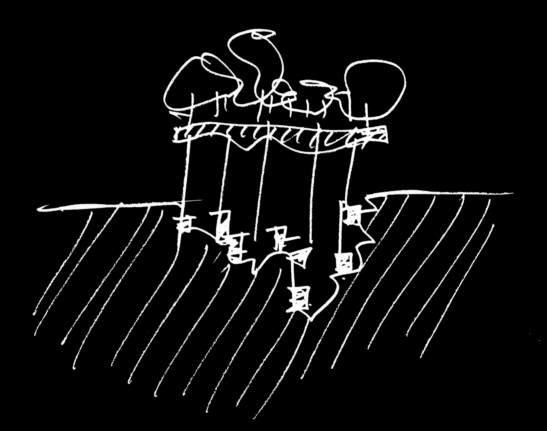

"Among the roads left open by the themes confronted in the Rogersian tradition, there remains the research of the prime architectural elements" (Manfredo Tafuri, *History of Italian Architecture 1944-1985*, Einaudi, Turin 1986)

The contest-experience in Italy deserves reflection in itself, irregardless of the fact that the author and the editor of this volume are Italian; therefore, paying particular attention to Perrault's proposals in our country could almost be legitimate, if it weren't too naively nationalistic and consequentially anti-contemporary in a moment in which not only the concept of globalization seems to have penetrated all consciousness, or nearly so, but above all, in a period in which it is strong and important to feel the sense of belonging to Europe. Therefore, banning local attention, it is true that the French architect's involvement in Italian competitions corresponds to a major portion of his most recent architectural productions, a central aspect of this monograph, entitled, as it were, "DPA. Recent works".

It is a matter of numerous occasions of great significance, some of which were to remain high-quality planning proposals of intelligence, regardless of their subsequent victory or not in contests —as is the case of the Juridical Citadel of Salerno[1], judged by David Chipperfield, for which Perrault had chosen another transparent, terraced blade to mark the city's skyline[2], or the case of the beautiful plan for the Gallery of Modern Art in

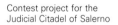

Contest project for the
Judicial Citadel of Salerno

Rome, won by the Swiss Diener & Diener[3], who proposed the encapsulation, without demolition, of the wing created by Luigi Cosenza (1965-1974)[4], a theme at the core of fierce debate in recent months— or their being held in stand-by, an impasse at the Oblomov without apparent reason, or because of purely political causes, as is frequently the case in our country. Only a small portion of this series of occasions has been realized —as with Piazza Gramsci in Cinisello Balsamo— or is in the process of realization —as seems to be the case with Piazza Garibaldi in Naples— or it is a matter of such recent assignments that have not yet left the blueprints, still undergoing scrutiny, even though they are surrounded by an aura of concrete practicability, as is the case with the foot-bridges of Palermo's ring road, the second of Perrault's direct assignments in Italy, after that of Piazza Garibaldi in Naples.

We are therefore proposing to analyze, through Perrault's Italian projects, the real occasions, as well those missed, of the Italian administration of architectural heritage, evidencing the planning solutions of his well-chosen design, which, in its various occasions, has never been exclusively influenced by history, but always by the complex geography of the locations. An attitude which, reassessed on Italian territory, despite its codifications, interpretations and far-fetched results, in a contemporary vision that is perhaps less "intellectually virtuosic", we like to bring back, perhaps with a bit of risk, to those important positions of architectural theory once belonging, for example, to Aldo Rossi, "the only 'leader' capable of continuously feeding a debate around his own work and his own figure, which ultimately invest the same concept of architecture", as per Manfredo Tafuri's conclusion that in Rossi's work, including his theory expressed in *L'architettura della città*[5], traced "the attempt to redefine urban science in agreement with the geography of the French school"[6]. And fundamentally, in Perrault's research, this aspect remains a priority in all scales of work.

Thus, not respecting the strong crisis, which seems to grip professionalism in Italian architecture for quite some time now, just when this seemed, with the new generations, to have completely evaded the academic influences and the overly theoretical rigidity of past years, Perrault, together with a series of other internationally renowned protagonists, including Fuksas, has recently returned to our country as a prophet, a leader of some very interesting projects in the process of realization. In addition to the newly completed square in Cinisello Balsamo[7], he is actually busy with the new Piazza Garibaldi in Naples, in the area adjacent to the Central Station, while in recent days[8], news has just arrived of his assignment of the work on the Central Pavilion of the Caldarelli Hospital. The South of Itlay seems paradoxically attracted to the severe and minimalist fascination of his language, almost as if it recognizes in the transparency of his containers, in history's absolute distance, the "less painful" life with the overcoming of "style" in favor of contemporaneity. Such is the case in Palermo, at the center of a noteworthy reawakening, which has commissioned him for a project of foot-bridges on the ring road[9]: "designed to connect places that have been divided by the passage of automobiles. In a peripheral neighborhood left quite fragmented, the *walks* could become a means of repossessing this part of the city"[10]. This Palermo assignment, emblematic of a series of broader initiatives pertaining to a plan aimed at recovering the Sicilian capital's waterfront[11], a visual perspective too long forgotten which, for years, has influenced an interpretation of the city's "inland" development, thereby modifying its original vocation as a seaport. The French architect, who will therefore design these vortical and colorful "elevated promenades" on the Viale Regione Siciliana, will also be the author, together with a team of international studios under the umbrella of the entrepreneurial group judging the competition, of Palermo's small-scale, automatic underground. For Perrault, the Palermo projects follow an ideal common thread, whether elevated or underground. "The city and the contemporary must find a relationship", says the French architect. "I believe that the key to this is constructing with respect to preexistence: in other words, without reverential fear. Otherwise, you risk making the historical center a kind of museum, leaving life, on the other hand, to be lived elsewhere". Themes of viability, of the relationship between the historical center and the peripheral areas, return in full force in yet another important project underway for Piazza Garibaldi in Naples, an assignment that goes well beyond the architectural renovation of the hypogeal area of the underground line —a true work of urban redesigning that will inevitably affect the entire neighborhood, the so-called "Five Stations", the beating heart of central Naples and the suburbs, a neuralgic node for all forms of transportation. An important occasion for the Neapolitan capital, which has already demonstrated intellectual daring in the past with its decision to assign its Directional Center to Kenzo Tange, and which anxiously awaits the realization of the new High-Speed Station by the casual and vibrant hand of Zaha Hadid[12]. With his faceted and perforated metal and glass forest that is to cover a new Piazza Garibaldi, beneath street-level and in contrast to the other part of the Piazza, planted with palms and marked, in its bipartition, by a completely redesigned arterial system, Perrault has intervened as a refined urbanist interested in recreating the location's geography with respect to its history.

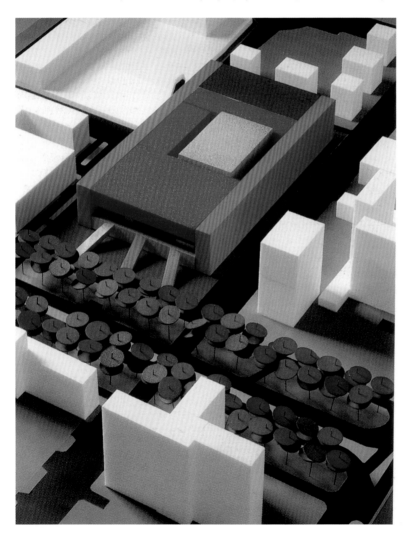

Model of the project for the contest for the new Congress Center of Rome

All things considered, Perrault has demonstrated a certain affection for the Neapolitan area and "for its density", as he himself indicated in 1998 with the project of restructuring the landscape of the Temple of Mitra, virtually an act of land art in the heart of the city, an opportunity to define a public space, a garden suspended over the excavation, indicating the presence of the archaeological site below, as well as the historical and geological stratification that characterizes the city's territory. The following year provided another, albeit suffered, encounter with Naples —the participation in the international contest held by TAV[13] for the new Afragola High-Speed Station in the area between northern Naples and Caserta. His impeccable project, a futuristic manta upon a sinuous system of curves on a plane, covered in shining solar panels on a multifunctional platform, although a candidate for victory until the last moment, had to settle for a well-earned second place in the contest.

But Perrault's professional relationship with Italy dates back to 1998, with the participation in four international competitions held in Rome, Venice, Milan and Naples. The French architect, recovered from the glory earned with the opening of the sites of the beautiful projects of the Aplix factory in Cellier-sur-Loire (1997-1999) and the Media Library of Vénissieux (1997-2001), opens for the contest for the Congress Center of Rome[14] with a new convention and multifunctional structure intended to "conceptually" substitute the emblematic building of the EUR, the congress building designed in 1938 by Adalberto Libera for the realization of the E42 exhibition area, commissioned by the Duke for the twentieth anniversary of the Fascist Revolution. Defined by Perrault himself as a "honeycomb"[15], his proposal for the new convention area is composed of a dynamically flowing glass box: continuously active on every level by day and by night, constituted by a series of suspended and floating parallelepipeds in a single, huge, "vibrant" principle container. The contest was ultimately won by Massimiliano Fuksas, just as, two years later, the other important Roman competition, for the headquarters of the Italian Space Agency. Here Perrault imagines a composition subdivided into four "binary glass walls", alternatively completed by geometrically regular, suspended boxes and spaces of green: glass-walled patios facing the dense fabric of the city. The Italian experience is not completed with these "nonaccomplishments", but proceeds, in the same year[16], with the participation in the international competition[17] held by the University Institute of Venice for its new home in a decentralized area —in contrast to that of the Tolentini, whose noble and historic structure was delicately yet significantly marked by the hand of Carlo Scarpa— the zone between land and sea, between port and railway, which is the area of the former Santa Martha Refrigeration Warehouses, on the so-called "outskirts" of the lagoon, between charming containers and wharfs. Here, Perrault's project, completely distant from the fragmentation proposed by the winner, that young master who was, too briefly, the Spanish Enric Miralles, planned the involvement of the wharf opposite the checkerboard-floored warehouses, a geometric base for the building's wings, conserved and cutout, like paper, in irregular forms, perforated by small apertures, almost like embrasures, ready to open up into unexpected loggias or into an ample entrance with a suspended catwalk. The interior, once again a large, transparent parallelepiped, would have interacted with four minor bodies in correspondence to the competition's functional requests. An independent, personal interpretation —despite its contemporaneity— of the compositional characteristics of the two "Roman" proposals; and once again, it is not history (and the Venetian proposal could have forcefully interjected) which dictates the direction of the program, but rather the geographic conditions of the location in its rarefied contextual fabric. The fascination with periphery and areas of disuse returns in the same year, but with a completely different theme, in the contest for ideas for the urban park of the Falck ex-industrial area in Sesto San Giovanni[18], in the region surrounding the city of Milan (see report in Chapter IV), where a grid system marked with various pathways and crossings becomes an instrument in the French designer's plans, treated as if it were a "construction material"[19], a position resumed shortly thereafter in the proposal for the restructuring of Piazza Gramsci in Cinisello Balsamo[20], recently concluded, where, in a visible, grilled, cement parterre, there are two diametrically opposed major modules, two pale podiums reachable by gently inclined ramps: upon one, the church of Saint Ambrogio and the churchyard, upon the other, a quadrangle of planted trees. Two rows of high, V-shaped lamps mark the limits of the Piazza itself. This is a work that can only be interpreted in the context of a broader plan for the reassessment of the city center, comprised of rare signs and few design elements that confer the Piazza a sense of suspended time and of sacredness, in this case, more closely resembling an agora than an acropolis.

Study for the renovation of Piazza Gramsci in Cinisello Balsamo, Milan

Contest project for the ex-Falck area in Sesto San Giovanni, Milan

Contest project for the new IUAV headquarters in Venice: general floor plan and a view of the university building

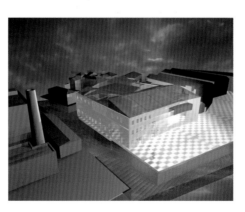

[1] One of the major works commissioned by the Municipality of Salerno in recent years is intended for the area of the former railway station. The general regulatory plan was assigned to Oriol Bohigas in 1998, whereas detailed plans allowed a series of international contests to be held. Among these, in addition to that for the Juridical Citadel, there is the contest for the Maritime Terminal, won by Zaha Hadid.

[2] Disassembled contour in sections later taken up for the Tower of the Hotel Nueva Diagonal in Barcelona (2001), in process of realization.

[3] F. Garofalo, *Progetto e destino. Otto architetti per l'ampliamento della Galleria Nazionale d'arte Moderna*, SACS, Turin, 2000.

[4] G. Cosenza, V. Bazzarini, *Luigi Cosenza. L'ampliamento della Galleria Nazionale d'Arte Moderna ed altre architetture 1929/1975*, CLEAN, Naples, 1988; G. Cosenza, F.D. Moccia, *Luigi Cosenza. L'opera completa*, Electa Napoli, Naples, 1987; F.D. Moccia, *Luigi Cosenza scritti e progetti di architettura*, CLEAN, Naples, 1994; C. De Sessa, *Luigi Cosenza. Razionalità senza dogmi*, Testo & Immagine, Turin, 2001.

[5] Ed. Marsilio, Padua, 1973.

[6] M. Tafuri, *Storia dell'architettura italiana 1944-1985*, Einaudi, Turin, 1986, p. 168.

[7] *L'Arca*, 144, January 2000, pp. 4-7.

[8] 13 May 2005.

[9] Actually: Plan for urban reassessment and elevated pedestrian links over the ring road.

[10] Perrault himself explained that together with the elevation's virtual animations, he showed a maquette of the project at the press conference, Palermo, February 2005.

[11] To this are added the small-scale underground judged by a team on which Perrault also participated, the plans for the thermal ventilator of Bellolampo by Studio Tange & Associates for Falck, the tourist fishing port of Presidiana in Cefalù by Mario Botta and the Wind Landscapes at Cinisi by the team composed of Vanderquand, Jambor, Menmier and Serafini.

[12] 'Zaha Hadid vince il concorso per l'Alta Velocità', in *La Repubblica*, October 2003.

[13] Treni Alta Velocità, one of the sixty companies that constitute the Trenitalia – Ferrovie dello Stato group.

[14] Competition won by Massimiliano Fuksas and presently in the process of realization.

[15] With Dominique Perrault, architect, Birkhauser-Actar, Barcelona, 1999.

[16] 1998.

[17] 'Concorso di progettazione per la nuova sede IUAV', appendix to *Casabella*, 665, 1998; S. Polano, P. Vetta, *10 progetti di concorso per la nuova sede IUAV*, Electa, Milan, 1999.

[18] *Concorso di idee per un parco urbano nell'area Falk a Sesto San Giovanni*, sponsored by the Town of Sesto San Giovanni, Milan, 1998.

[19] *Dominique Perrault*, Electa, 2000, p. 86.

[20] International contest sponsored by the Town of Cinisello Balsamo in 1998.

Piazza Gramsci
Cinisello Balsamo, Milan, 1999-2004

In 1999, the town of Cinisello Balsamo called a contest for the restructuring of the historic Piazza Gramsci, open to all professionals residing in the European Union. The contest's jury, presided over by Cesare Sevan and constituted of reputable personalities, such as Gae Aulenti, Cino Zucchi and Roberto Camagni, decreed as winner the significantly entitled project, "Gramsci philosopher" by Dominique Perrault. Once again, the French architect is faced with historical issues, in this case, those of a Piazza and an 18th century church, the church of Saint Ambrogio. Perrault does not deny his position with respect to history, preferring rather the geography of the location, through a "minimalist" project that highlights the new structures next to the preexisting. Since the end of the 18th century, the Piazza has been conceived of as the heart of city life, the importance of which is further sustained by the presence of the church of Saint Ambrogio and by the commercial activity carried out there with the open market. "La Perla", so named because of its white, oval form, has undergone numerous modifications over the course of time, until assuming the present form which we know today, characterized by a neutral space with imprinted cement flooring, reserved to pedestrians and lawns, physically separated from the roadway. The work's principle objectives, as determined by the town, are to create a more accessible and utilizable space for residents, simultaneously respecting the historical buildings and the commercial activity. Perrault intended Piazza Gramsci as a meeting and gathering place; his project provided for the creation of two elevated poles of attraction: the church and the churchyard on one end, and the lawns on the other. The churchyard, already elevated approximately 80 cm from the Piazza's level, was extended, while the church benefits from a new illumination, designed to enhance its presence. The pedestrian zone (approximately 13,000 m²), elevated from the road surface, hosts the Piazza's green heart within, extending over an area of approximately 2,000 m². The two areas are paved with two different materials: light grey imprinted cement and white Carrara marble, covering the two islands that emerge: the green pole and the churchyard. This chromatic diversity confers greater presence to two central poles, while the peripheral streets, such as Martiri di Belfiore, Frova and Martiri di Fossoli, are assimilated to the Piazza through the use of the same pavement. The illumination, purposefully planned by Perrault, was distributed from above through the application of one- and two-armed metal poles ending in a diffuser and from below by horizontal beams of light directed at the garden. The church is illuminated by projectors with special lenses. (C.M.)

View of the square before
and after the renovation
project

Contest table: sections
and floor plans of the area

View of the completed
square and detail of the
"procession" of Y-shaped
lamps designed by Perrault

View of the square:
in the upper frame,
the checkerboard planting

Project and glimpse
of the completed work

The tiered area of the square
facing the churchyard and,
in the background, the
Church of Saint Ambrogio

Extension of the National Gallery
of Modern Art
Rome, 2000

In 2000, Italian Minister for Cultural Assets and Activities holds an international contest for the project of extending the National Gallery of Modern Art in Rome, which requires the creation of new exhibition spaces: an auditorium, laboratories and new offices. The jury, composed of authoritative figures of contemporary architecture and art, was presided over by Sandra Pinto, Superintendent of Contemporary Art. Of the numerous architects as candidates for the project, only eight were called upon to develop a preliminary project, which could provide the details of the means and costs of the work. The winning project was that of the Swiss studio Diener & Diener, which required a major alteration of the antique architectural arrangement. The desire for renovation clashed, in this case, with the desire to prize and conserve the building's most antique aspect, bringing rise to great debate. The project's first draft was, in fact, favorable to the demolition of the addition already created by the rationalist architect Luigi Cosenza, flanking the main building of classic mould by architect Bazzani. The necessity to define a single organism, both functionally as well as architecturally, caused many architects to hold as necessary the dem-olition of the Cosenza wing, while others were inclined to envision a structure that could encompass the long sleeve of reinforced cement. Dominique Perrault presented a project that would integrate the Cosenza pavilion within the new building, through a connection created by a linear metallic structure. The French architect's vision of the new structure was that of a prism, extending over 8,000 square meters, whose remarkable scenic effect is largely enhanced by the choice of a translucent material such as a white filtering glass. Two panes of opal glass, enameled or transparent, compose the face, extending to the roof; materials such as polycarbonate, Plexiglas and perforated aluminum, inserted between the glass panes, would serve to filter the light, the element of primary importance in this specific context. The museum's new entrance also serves as an access to the auditorium, while three different levels host the various functional areas: the sublevel is intended for utilities, also housing a storage room and areas exclusively for employee use; the ground floor is completely open to public service, while the first floor houses laboratories and administrative offices. (C.M.)

General floor plan of the
intervention inserted into
the context of the park
of Villa Borghese

View of the Gallery's new
exhibit space

Detail of the contest model

Plan of the ground floor
and first floor

View of the model from
above, with the insertion
of the luminous box of the
new work, as it dialogues
with the pre-existing

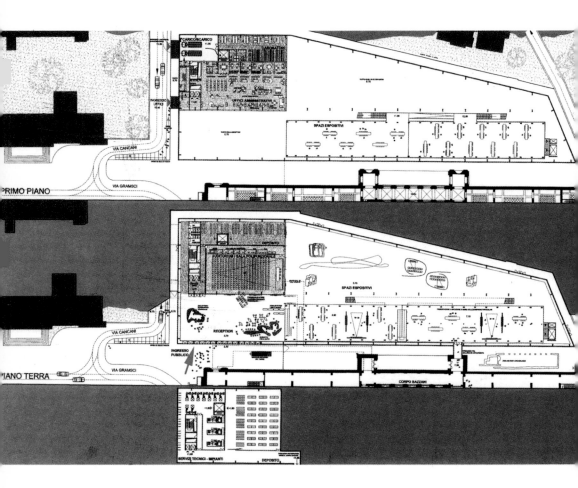

High-Speed Station TAV
Naples-Afragola, 1999

The plan for the high-speed station of Afragola was commissioned by TAV (Treno Alta Velocità), which held an international architectural contest in 1999. The jury, presided by architect Oriol Bohigas, selected ten plans in the second phase from a bouquet of illustrious exponents of contemporary architecture, among whom Zaha Hadid emerged victorious with his bridge-gallery suspended upon an ironclad system. The architectural intervention was necessary to create an efficient transportation center, within which the functions strictly pertaining to the railway could be integrated with commercial and recreational activities, as in the most modern of European stations. For Perrault, the Neapolitan station would have been well adapted to becoming an "urban loggia", whose structure is characterized by an undulating movement, adapted to the plot's natural topography. The architectural complex is composed of three levels: the sublevel is intended for storage and technical use; the ground level is reserved for vehicular circulation pertaining to transfers between trains and other forms of public and private transportation; finally, the first floor, at an elevation of nine meters,

serves as a center for commercial activities, complete with cultural spaces and restaurants. This stratification in levels does not negate the uniformity of the complex, guaranteed to be absent of sharp contrasts between the horizontal and vertical planes. The result is that of a large open space, permeable from one end to the other through the numerous entrances situated along its perimeter. The covering is concretized in a series of curves on a plane that amplify the entire structure's effect of lightness; the surface is paved with solar panels, presenting ample apertures, which in turn allow the infiltration of natural light. The station's only enclosed spaces are constituted by cylindrical volumes, at full height or shorter, which Perrault defines as "big kiosks, flexible in form and position" intended for hosting commercial activity, postal services, banks and receptive structures. Perrault's proposal reveals his research of a constant rapport with the territory, with the location's geography, even in this context, where a variety of trees outlines strips of external car parks, with each point of the loggia offering the eyes a splendid view of Vesuvius. (C.M.)

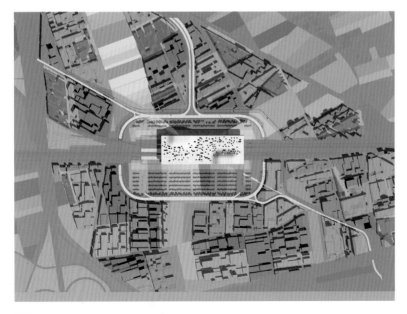

General floor plan: the contest proposal inserted into the territorial context

Comprehensive view of the
station with sourroundings

Longitudinal section

Comprehensive view:
the station's main façade,
characterized by the double
"clevil fish", a wave that
becomes an access ramp
in the central area

Next pages
The intervention with
the area behind station
dedicated to parking

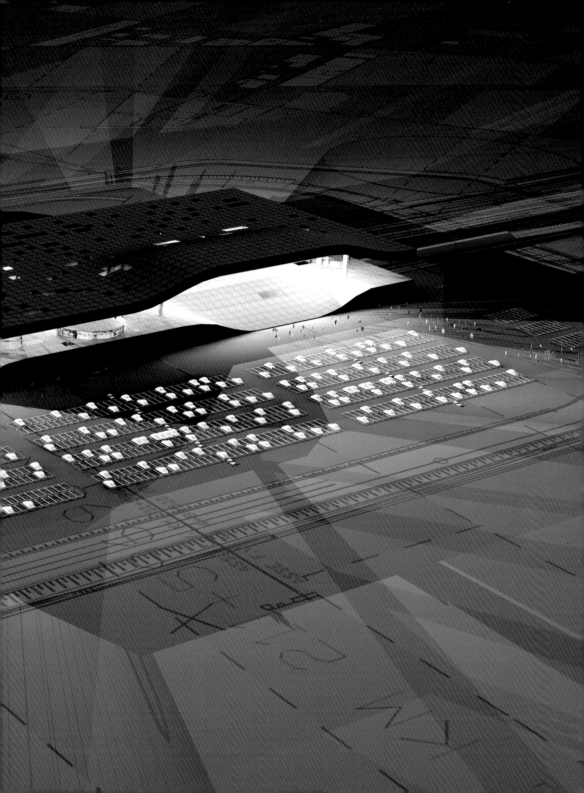

Interior view: one
of the station's platform

Top view of the station
characterized by the
suggestive wave-like
covering

Renovation of Piazza Garibaldi
Naples, 2004-2008

Piazza Garibaldi in Naples is certainly one of the city's most neuralgic zones, an epicenter of Neapolitan movement and vivacity and a strategically important location. Its extension (64,000 m²), greater than the other Neapolitan piazzas, requires an intervention of reorganization that also takes into consideration the logistical needs that this area attempts to satisfy. In fact, it comprises the connective ring between the historical city and the newer section, the neuralgic node of exchange among the principal means of public transportation between the city and the suburbs. For too long it has been suffering from problems of congestion due to the immediate proximity of five stations: the central railway station, the two underground stations of the 1 and 2 lines, the Circumvesuvian Station and the soon-to-arrive high-speed station designed by Zaha Hadid. For this reason, global intervention was made a priority, aiming for a "total" reorganization of the Five Stations Neighborhood.

Dominique Perrault is the winner of the contest held by the city, and in redesigning the old urban layout he will have to consider the needs of the owners of the plot: the city of Naples and the Ferrovie dello Stato. In fact, the intervention's all-encompassing nature also includes, in addition to architectural restructuring, the reinforcement of the transportation resources, whose efficiency will largely be determined by the development of the future neighborhood. This operation will be realizable through: the optimization of the public transportation network through an improvement of user-accessibility of the services, which will serve to lighten, as much as possible, the flow of vehicles entering the city, a new organization of vehicular traffic in the north-south zone, the restructuring of the existing stations and the provision of a network of pedestrian connections that guarantees an interaction with the new metropolitan structures. The Five Stations Neighborhood is also the neighborhood of piazzas, with the Piazza della Stazione Centrale, the Piazza dei Giardini, the Piazza dell'Alta Velocità and the two satellite piazzas, as well as the Piazza Principe Umberto and the Piazza Nolana, to which the French architect must confer an organized aspect for the rational integration between the zone of pedestrian traffic and that of vehicular traffic. Thus, the vehicles arriving in the city's center will be directed along a two-lane route in one direction, which crosses the piazza towards the Central Station; the vehicles arriving from the east will follow Corso A. Lucci, which takes them along the side of the Central Station. The piazza's plot will be divided into two sides by a central route: north and south, establishing circulation in a double ring that encompasses the blocks contiguous to the two sides. This operation of the reorganization of the traffic zone will not only provide a correct viability, but, above all, the revitalization and reassessment of some of the presently stagnated peripheral areas.

From a strictly architectural point of view, Perrault has focalized his attention on a concept of asymmetry, imagining the space partitioned into an open and a protected area: the northern part is intended for an area of gardens, a playground and resting spaces, comprehensive of the access routes and the network of underground services, guaranteed in their strategic points; the southern part is constituted by a covered space that protects a hypogeal piazza. The former is also an open-air gallery and walkway, in this context becoming an entrance to a subterranean, parallel city, solidly integrated with the existing one. Perrault's objective is to "create new architecture that redesigns the geography of locations". He has planned separate spaces, capable of interacting through the exchange of natural light originating in the transparent gallery, a home for commercial centers, shops, cafés and restaurants. Thanks to a large perforation at ground-level, different and unexpected views of the ensemble are opened up: from the Piazza Alta towards the gallery and from the gallery upwards. Despite the radical changes, the architect demonstrates his intention to conserve as well as to exploit the piazza's identity, hence the idea of planning a large covering, a *manta* enclosing both Garibaldi 1 and 2, is conceived and developed as the continuation of the existing Central Station, complete with a tower and a large canopy. The new structure attempts to conserve the dimensional connotation of the existing structure while distinguishing itself from it through the use of materials and structural logic. It does not exceed the height of the buildings adjacent to the piazza, and although it rises up from the ground, it does so in just proportion as perceived by the public in the piazza. The project aims to create a *promenade* piazza, necessary for the intersection of the city's essential functions, but at the same time crucial for the assessment of Piazza Garibaldi as a "piazza in progress". (C.M.)

Two views of the contest model
with the renovation of Piazza
Garibaldi

View of the square with shelters
for waiting, the ample covering
for the underground level,
the stairway providing access
to the subway

Next pages
The proposal for the
renovation Piazza Garibaldi,
partially planted and partially
covered by the structure
of metallic mesh

System of Foot-bridges
on Viale della Regione Siciliana
Palermo, 2004-2006

Perrault's most recent project in Italy is the one destined for the city of Palermo, which plans for the creation of foot-bridges on the ring road. The work will begin by 2006, restituting a sense of futurism to this area of the city.

This large plan arises from the need to unite the two extreme edges of the city, separated today by the ring road: Piazza Einstein and Piazzale Lennon. The two peripheral zones will therefore become the point of departure for this urban planning; not merely reinserted, they will acquire a new identity. According to Perrault, "the walkways could become a means of reclaiming this part of the city [...] re-establishing a dialogue, a connection between locations that are currently separated".

The new system of pedestrian crossings is composed of four foot-bridges from 150 to 500 meters in length, with a total area of 6,000 square meters and crossing times that vary from approximately four to fifteen minutes, depending on the respective distances. The colors of each foot-bridge will also vary: red, blue, green and pink. This new system will provide the advantage of easy access to public transportation and a greater fluidization of traffic through the elimination of a number of pedestrian-traffic lights currently in use. The work will be carried out in various distinct phases: the first phase is dedicated to the construction of two foot-bridges, red and blue, of 300 meters each, connecting the car park and access to the public transportation of Piazzale Lennon, with a park area on the upper side of the ring road (next to the rotary of Via Leonardo da Vinci, Piazza Einstein and Via Giorgione). During the second phase, the blue bridge will be prolonged to Mt. Agip and the future bus stop. In conclusion, the other two foot-bridges, the yellow and the pink, will be constructed: one over the rotary of Via Leonardo da Vinci and the other connecting the preceding foot-bridges and extending to Via Uditore. The foot-bridges are constructed of a sort of pyramidal grid, with some sections covered in a perforated metallic grill that creates particular visual effects depending on how it is struck by light. The three bridges were intended as rest areas and are connected to the ground through stairs and elevators; the flooring is completely in wood. (C.M.)

View of the project inserted
into the urban context

Nocturnal rendering:
the luminous foot-bridge
in proximity of the ring-road

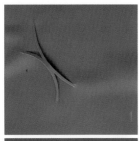

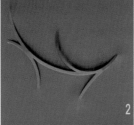

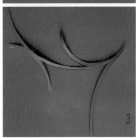

Study-diagram referring
to the three phases
of realization

Day and night for one
of the steel-structured
walkways

Chapter IV

Geography like Analitical Matrix predominant on History

The French school has always favored geography over history as an analytical instrument, and as we have already mentioned, urban geography[1] represents one of the central elements in Perrault's research. The projects on a territorial scale, those that have involved large urban and extra-urban areas, represent, in their variation of scale, the emblematic cases of a planning approach that can be traced even in the works of lesser dimension, which establishes a relationship with context and its appropriation as a primary theme in the planning process.

The notion of geography is therefore comparable to that of context. This is not conceived exclusively in its acceptance of the ensemble of entities and historical preexistences, which we Italians are foremost in indulging, but according to a broader, more complex vision, contaminated by anthropology, sociology, agronomy and geology, which allows greater liberty of programmatic action. "It is possible to manipulate the context as if it were a material," states the author. The scale may change, but the approach of the problem remains the same. A location can be interpreted from the most varied points of view, just as the analysis of the skyline and its modification can represent a planning choice, and it is worth reasoning in plans, but also in flows and volumes, in lines of level.

Since 2000, numerous studies of territorial and urban renovation have been conducted by DPA, some of which[2] are presently in the process of realization, such as the tourist area in Tenerife, known as "Las Teresitas" and the Manzanares Athletic Park in Madrid. The former concerns the realization of the new Olympic Tennis Center within a park area of 80,000 m^2 and is a theme (that of sports areas) to which Perrault is certainly no stranger. In addition to the Berlin project of the Olympic Velodrome and Swimming Pool (1992-1998), the French architect already had the occasion of confronting the theme of "athletics" in 1993 with the Grand Stade di Melun-Sénart[3], followed by the Montigalà Athletic Complex in Badalona (1997) in the suburbs of Barcelona, presently in the process of realization and, most recently, his invitation for a study of the Paris 2017 village, in the case that the French capital is chosen for the next Olympics. While the stadium of Melun strongly represents a refined structural technology tied to a profound territorial design, penetrating, as in Berlin, part of the large field marked by traversing roads in the vocation of permanence, in Badalona the author, despite his confirmation of the idea of excavation as a substantial one in the stadium's conception, seems more interested in the "nomadic" aspect of architectural manufacture, such that Gilles de Bure[4], recent author of the passionate monograph of Perrault's work, examines the question of defining this work by providing a fascinating description: "the tent

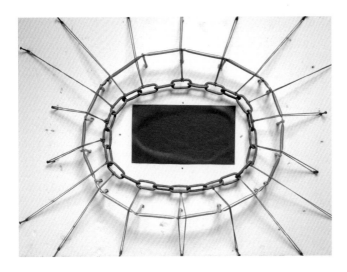

Montigalà athletic complex in Badalona and detail of the stadium

of a nomad? the net of a fisherman stretched over a forest of pylons? a giant insect, whose membranes seem to expand to infinity?". Once again, territorial design, in numerous other occasions of planning on the theme of the urban park (i.e. a place characterized by lawns and gardens and services, but without specific athletic structures) has paved the way for a 1998 project proposed for the contest for the ex-Falck area of Sesto San Giovanni. Here, Perrault superimposes the location's natural vocation —even from the perspective of maintaining the already present arboreal essence— with a strong mark of planning involving the artificialization of the area, implementing the concept of a grid, here similar to a chessboard, in his so-called incarnation of a "elastic method of realization, open and flexible", just as would concern a complex urban program. Along the same line, DPA has intervened in the project for the Botanic Garden of Chevreloup in Versailles (2000-2002), whereas it deviates from this compositional formula in the programmatic organization of the touristic center, "Las Teresitas", where the key was to adapt to the location's topography, working with the context, respecting the "empty" areas and diversifying the types of interventions. But here the chessboard has made way for the identification of completely redesigned functional areas, like the Ciudadela, and the Park (even here with a stadium and an area intended for sports) and, primarily, in the redesigning of the beach —once again the artificialization of the landscape— and above all of the rocks, declared by the author himself as a Smithsonian[5] memorial Land Art installation. A refined citation, while possible in a planning condition like that of the Spanish island, is certainly not repeatable in metropolitan contexts like those of Amsterdam, Helsinki, Vienna, Rome or Hamburg, cities in which Perrault has conducted numerous studies of urban redesign. A 200 meter-high tower with a zigzagging glass surface will mark the skyline of Donau[6], for example, the Viennese area that is the object of DPA's study for a general regulatory plan that will be accompanied by the redesigning of the entire area of the river-

Botanic park of Chevreloup

Renovation of the beach
of Las Teresitas in Tenerife

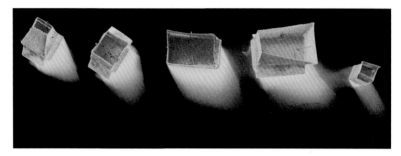

Model of the project
for the urban renovation
of the port of Helsinki

front on the Danube with the opening of a collective space, a square, that is in turn an extension of the neighborhood according to a new language, far removed from that of fin de siècle Vienna, alternatingly baroque, eclectic and secessionist. Again, the theme of the waterfront returns in the restructuring of the port area of Helsinki (2000-2001), as in the case of Hamburg with the Promenade du Jungfernstieg, the mark of land art on water, it could perhaps be defined as a "floating island", to use the words of the author in a sketch of the study, a project that earned Perrault recognition in the 2003 contest. Similarly, the study for the area of the Schipol Airport at Haarlemmermeer (Amsterdam) redefines the complexity of the relationship between a landscape of polder and the two cities (Amsterdam and L'Aia), historically joined by an artery that was interrupted by the airport itself, through a suspended and distributional "Living Bridge" applying an element of crossing, destined to complete the new airport with hotels, offices and services. Finally, the participation in the contest for ideas for the "Emperor Justinian" area[7] in the south of Rome, in the proximity of the historic Saint Paul Basilica, represented an occasion to approach the monumental city in an area which, although not suburban, is spangled with empty lots, undeveloped even as parks, with no services and cut off from important arteries of viability. Here, the elaboration of a master plan would have permitted the assessment of a strategy for intervention in the realization of a system of spaces of public interest and the appropriate means of substitution, integration or densification of the already existing buildings. Perrault declaredly decided on a vision of the neighborhood as an equipped residential park, where the Justinian Emperor Avenue is transformed into a green axis —an equipped island in the complex system of relationships of Rome.

'Floating island' study-sketch for the Promenade Jungfernstieg of Hamburg

Urban transformation of Danau City, Vienna

[1] P. George, *Geografia e sociologia*, il Saggiatore, Milan, 1976, p. 22; *Sociologie et Géographie*, Presses Universitaires de France, Paris, 1966.

[2] Obtained following the victory in international contests, such as, for example, the touristic complex "Las Teresitas" and the Athletic Park on the Manzanares River, in addition to direct commissions, as in the case of the studies for Haarlemmermeer and Helsinki.

[3] Contest won, but without follow-up. Successively, Perrault also works on the stadiums of Zurich, Lille and Marseilles.

[4] G. de Bure, *Dominique Perrault*, Terrail Vilo, Paris, 2004.

[5] Peter (1923) and Alison (1928) Smithson, Anglo-Saxon architects joining in association in 1950, adhere to the Team X, later becoming among the leaders of Brutalism. Their architecture is characterized by a "technological minimalism", strongly characterized by the relationship with locations and territory. Among their projects are the Hunstanton Secondary School, Norfolk (1949-1954), The House of the Future exhibition (1956 at the Ideal Home Show), Garden Building, St Hilda's College, Oxford (1968); Robin Hood Gardens housing complex, Poplar, East London (1969-1972); the headquarters of The Economist, Piccadilly, London (1959-1965); buildings for the University of Bath: the School of Architecture and Engineering (1988)

[6] A direct assignment from 2004, whose conclusion is expected in 2008.

[7] Planning-contest in two phases, held by the City of Rome: *Segni di qualità: Giustiniano imperatore*. The examination board, composed of Alessandro Anselmi, Paolo Berdini, Andrea Branzi, Pippo Ciorra, Gabriella Raggi, Flora Ruchat-Roncati, Andrea Magnanelli, Fausto Gargaglia and Lucio Passarelli selected five groups for the first phase: Stefano Cordeschi, Jean Pierre Durig, Insula Architettura e Ingegneria, Dominique Perrault, Frits Van Dongen - CIE architekten. Perrault took 3rd place.

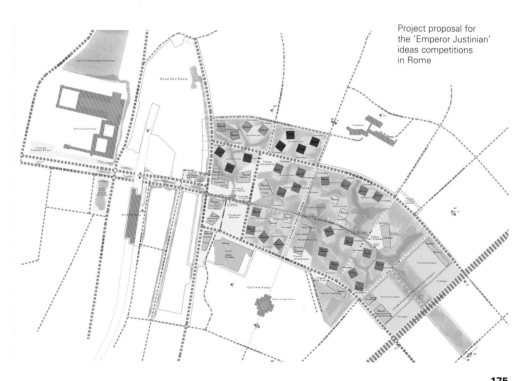

Project proposal for the 'Emperor Justinian' ideas competitions in Rome

Falck Area
Sesto San Giovanni, Milan, 1998

The contest held in 1998 for the reassessment of the former industrial area of Sesto San Giovanni was born out of the necessity to resuscitate the city's economy and image. The plan intends to give the entire area a new identity, through the creation of an urban complex, furnished with streets, neighborhoods, squares and a large unitary park. The series of proposed autonomous territorial interventions, integrated amongst themselves, has acquired some degree of realization, each individual work generated through an interpretation of the entire zone's industrial past; in fact, many of the new constructions coexist with some parts of the old industrial buildings. The contest's sponsors, the Town of Sesto and the Falck Group, made their selection of the winning project among the proposals of 111 Italian and 57 foreign architects. The park planned by Dominique Perrault is integrated in an urban space organized in a grid, subdivided into quadrangular blocks in a system composed of small "modules" of approximately 100 m x 100 m, which host the various structures and essences and would ideally be realized in multiple phases. The total area of the intervention is 480,000 m² and includes newly created parks and gardens spaces next to preexisting vegetation. (C.M.)

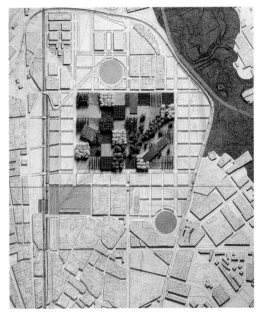

General floor plan of the work inserted into the urban context

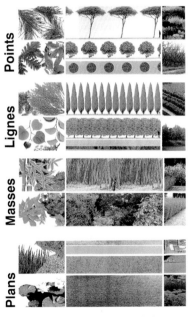

Contest table with the essential elements chosen for the urban park

Contest table: plan of the intervention

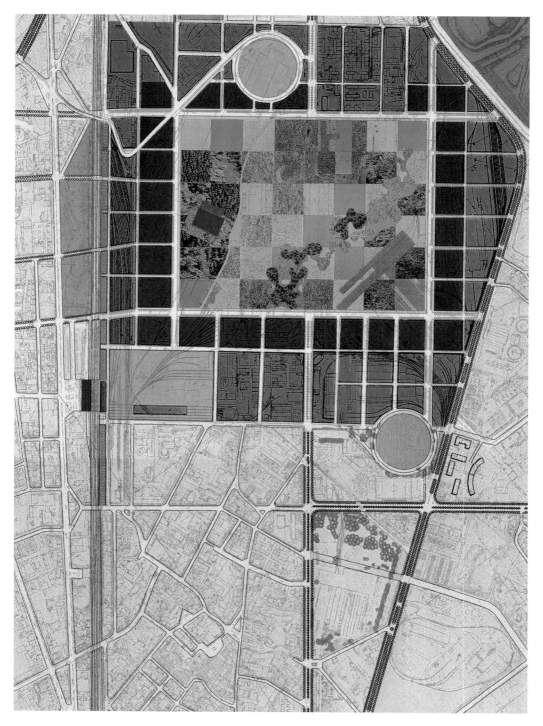

Contest table with
photomontage and present
state of the ex-industrial
area

Contest table: rendering
with suspended passage

Present state
of the ex-industrial area

Renovation of the beach of Las Teresitas and construction of a hotel

Santa Cruz de Tenerife, 2002-2006

The realization of this Spanish beach affords Dominique Perrault the opportunity to intervene in a non-urbanized, completely natural context. Winner of the contest held in 2002, the French architect proposes to intervene in absolute respect of the territory's morphology, transforming the zone of the former "Ciudadela" into a new tourist center. His project provides for the realization of a new beach, a rocky strip, a tourist port and a diversified system along the entire cost intended for commercial, conferential, and athletic activities —including a large football stadium immersed in the park above the citadel— as well recreational facilities, including theme parks.

The semicircular beach follows the relief of the surrounding topography and is partially covered by a metal structure that forms a large, undulating sail, practically vibrating, so light that it seems to follow the wind in movement. The use of metal, even in this context, confirms Perrault's preference for materials that allow the creation of structural skeletons, even flexible ones, animated by movements that are clearly perceptible in their visual impact. In a zone which is elevated from the beach, there is the central nucleus of the entire tourist complex: a sort of fortress enclosing a tropical oasis. The luxury hotel, comprised of 500 rooms, develops horizontally, facing the sea; next to it is the recreation center, pool, miniature golf, spa and an ample car park.

Las Teresitas is conceived as the sum of different cultures, the neuralgic center of ethno-cultural diversity in its encounter in Tenerife —Spanish island with African and Arab heart— as is the case on the mythical beaches of Copacabana, Malibù and Miami. Avenues of towering palms run along the mountainous path and along the beach, shading the pedestrian promenade. Rotaries were intended for the zone of vehicular traffic, in addition to specific relief points, intended to facilitate its flow. The tourist port, not intended for the mooring of ships, but rather as the archetype of a landing, becomes a characteristic part of the bathing area. Nature becomes architecture in this artificialized landscape, where the sand, directly imported from the Sahara, the "installed" rocks, the mountains surrounding the beach and the green of the natural and implanted tropical plants become the prime materials along with the metal and cement of the structures. (C.M.)

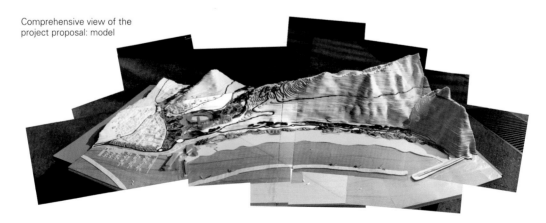

Comprehensive view of the project proposal: model

Comprehensive view
of the coast: photomontage

Study-sketch

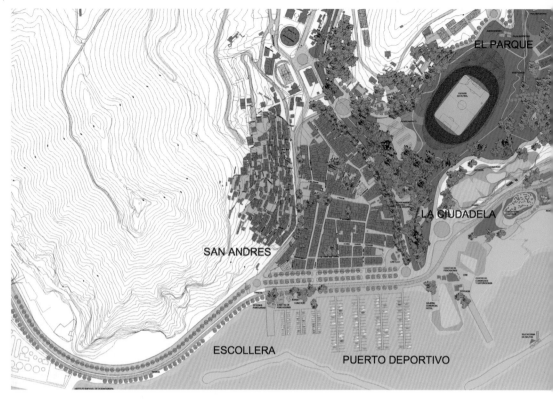

General floor plan
of the intervention and
comprehensive view

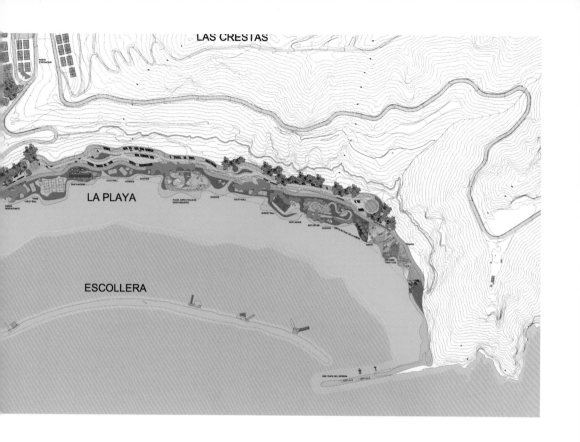

LAS CRESTAS

LA PLAYA

ESCOLLERA

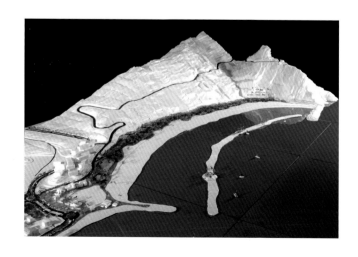

Details and general views
of the hotel structure
intended for the touristic
center

View of the beach from
the hotel

The large hotel structure
wrapped in its cloak
of metallic mesh

The project of renovation of the terraces and walkways along the coast

Planning-project for the Area of Amsterdam Schiphol Airport, Haarlemmermeer

The Netherlands, 2000-2002

A series of images
of the model inserted
into the territorial context

The urban study of the territorial sector located to the north-east of the Schiphol airport in Amsterdam involves an area of 1,300 by 80 meters.

A functional route intercalated by three "sequences" of completely distinct connotation: the Hotel Accor, the Golf Hotel to the north and finally, the actual airport, with the headquarters of KLM, in the area extending to the south of the "corridor".

The project calls for the realization of a sequential weave with a series of "addresses" identifiable along the route. This route, conceived as the structural axis connecting the various functions, is absolutely flexible and infinitely extendable in its development, continually becoming more of an urban strip, as states Perrault, an inhabited bridge —a "Living Bridge"— that, because of its width, could progressively host offices, restaurants and conference centers, as well as areas dedicated to free-time.

The planning of this area has highlighted the connective line between Amsterdam and the airport which, until the construction of the A9 motorway, constituted the principal link between Amsterdam and the Hague.

Upon this historic axis, a simple system of public transportation is foreseen that consists of the creation of a bus line and an underground.

The construction of the Accor site and the services tied to the motorway network and its projects have necessitated the insertion of a vertical building, highly visible from the new corridor-strip as well as from the motorways. (G.C.)

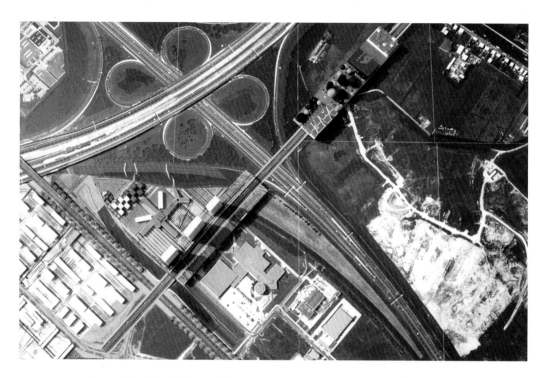

View of the model: the
functional stick as a mark
upon the territory

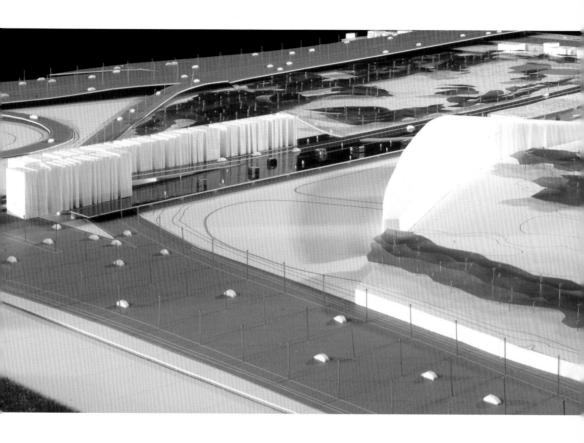

Restructuring of the Promenade du Jungfernstieg
Hamburg, 2002

The contest by invitation, reserved to ten participants, which was held in May 2002 for the architectural restructuring of the Jungfernstieg, one of the principle commercial streets of Hamburg's center, required the formation of a team composed of architects, landscapers and artists, with the precise intention of substituting the urban landscape and illumination, of constructing a new wharf with a restaurant and bar and of restructuring the preexisting pavilions, also providing for an artistic installation.

The project, conceived by Dominique Perrault with the collaboration of the landscaping firm Plannungs-büro Decker of Bottrop-Kirchhellen and of the artist Klaus Kumrow of Hamburg, represents an interdisciplinary urban study and a new window on the landscape. Before flowing into the Elba, which splits here into two branches, the Alster River becomes a large basin called Aussenalster, separated from a second and smaller one, the Binnenalster, by a narrow strip of land crossed by roadways. The Jungfernstieg opens up completely to the Binnenalster with a silhouette strongly characterized by the imposing presence of its historic buildings.

In this perspective, the project attempts to preserve the character of the Jungfernstieg and to follow, so to speak, the qualities of the place, its geography and its history.

The idea behind the project is to redefine the landscape, in such a special position, respecting the preexisting urban fabric and reutilizing the geometry of the urban plot.

To establish the geography of the place and clarify the functioning of the entire Jungfernstieg, a homogeneous parterre is extended from the water to the constructions, lending a unity to the ensemble. Hence, a place is created where different areas can be distinguished.

First of all, the act of extending the commercial strip flanking the Bergerhauser provides great comfort to its users, encouraging them to remain on the new terrace overlooking the water. The underground entrances acquire a new, shining metallic skin, while the lighting systems, also metallic, emit light according to a scheme which accents verticality.

The traffic in the central area, intended for public transportation, is greatly reduced, as it is channeled into other arteries. In addition, numerous pedestrian crosswalks allow a simpler and more direct connection between the mirror of water and the commercial strip.

The zone of passage on the water, reserved for pedestrians and bicyclists, provides a protected pathway within the city, delineated by a boulevard of linden trees, which by day signals a direction and by night, adequately illuminated, seems to shine like the surface of the water. From the preexisting Alsterpavillion, the passage continues uninterruptedly, even to the view, proposing a new landscape.

At the level of the water, far from the bank, the dock occupies a singular position. The wharf defines a clear rapport with the city. Hiding its secrets beneath the water and floating freely, it creates the illusion of crowning the landscape, consciously distancing Alster's navigational activity from the passage, providing a cover suspended on the water, offering a place of rest to navigators. In addition, the openings along the pontoon play with the sky's reflection on the water, providing special glimpses. The new dock thereby allows an ulterior view of the landscape, this time in the direction of the city and of the new port.

The colors of the sky, the water and the red-white city play an important role in the project, as they define an image, a landscape painted by an artist. Thus, the white wharf "establishes a vibration, like a brightness or a reflection, which nourishes the colors of the water and the sky".

The light upon the distant white material arouses this poetry. (G.C.)

Aereal view
of the intervention
in the urban context

General floor plan

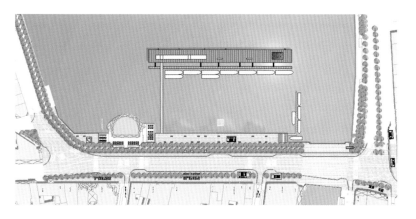

Intervention by the artist
Klaus Kumrow for the
contest for the renovation
of Promenade
du Jungfernstieg

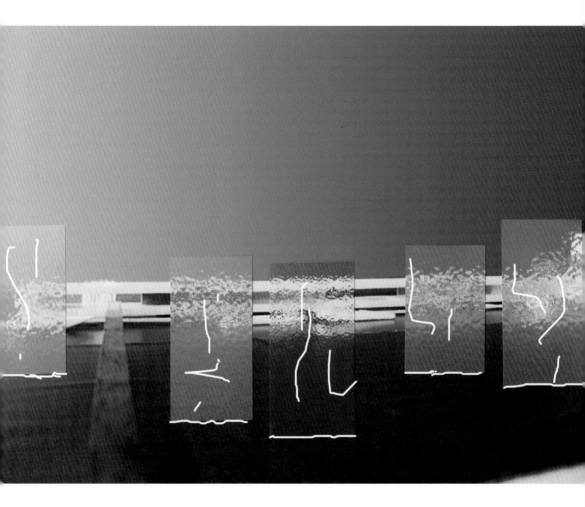

The Promenade as a model,
inserted into the urban context

Olimpic Tennis Center
in the Manzanares River Park
Madrid, 2002-2007

In April 2002, the city council of Madrid invites some of the world's most important planners —Norman Foster, Peter Eisenman, Jacques Herzog-Pierre De Meuron, Rem Koolhaas, José Antonio Martínez Lapeña-Elías Torres, Juan Navarro Baldeweg, Dominique Perrault and Kazuyo Sejima-Ryue Nishizawa— to participate in an international competition for the Parque Lineal del Río Manzanares in Madrid, with hopes of hosting the 2012 Olympic games. This challenge to rebalance the territory is no more than the continuation of the project of the Linear Park of the Meleti, created in 2003 by architect Ricardo Bofill. Situated in Usera, the capital's southern zone, the ex-laborer's neighborhood of San Fermín, which Bofill's park separated from the nearby M-30, the new work hopes to improve the conditions of this peripheral area, the quality of Madrid's landscape, as well as providing a balance between the city's southern and northern zones.

Dominique Perrault's winning plans are based on a sustainable architecture merged with high technology. The ideation of the athletic center in the park along the Manzanares River is a chance to simultaneously confront some heterogeneous themes already present to a large extent in Perrault's projects". Constructing a landscape, installing an architecture, superimposing two worlds" are three different intentions that together may bring success to a unitary functional system.

The desire to construct a landscape is expressed in the extrapolation of models of the location itself, taking advantage of the elements that characterize it, as in the case of the element water which, in its expansion, defines a large horizontal plane of reference, a great natural mirror. What we are describing is an ecological lake (recycled water) surrounded by 80,000 square meters of green nature, arid or lush depending on the irrigation, where passages along walkways, jetties and squares/terraces unfold, liberating broad views of the entire landscape.

The concepts of clothing and magic boxes surround these multifunctional athletic buildings. The container opens and closes, each time according to the func-

Comprehensive view:
the large box for tennis
and the park

tions required of the athletic complex, creating a mutable profile, alive in the landscape. This mobile and vibrant metallic skin filters the sun, breaks the force of the wind and protects the hall's public space like a light enclosure. The magic box that contains the athletic pavilions is composed of the stratification of various materials: filtering, reflecting and opaque, shimmering with light during the day, mysterious and lavish by night, like a theatrical scene. The main pavilion, housing three arenas with capacities of 12,000, 3,500 and 2,500 spectators respectively, can be completely closed. The lateral area is transformed through curtains that, when raised, permit the flow of visitors, sliding panels along the technical facilities area and large shutters to the west, offering protection from the setting sun.

Finally, the idea of "superimposing two worlds", upon which the distribution of the entire project is constructed, allows for a casual and dynamic use, avoiding an accumulation of the masses: at the water's level, there will be paths and accesses for athletes and technicians, whereas the public will enter from above.

The functions of training, education and welcoming of the athletes and VIPs and the media, the technical installations, the athletic complex of 11 covered fields and the equipment reserved for the events are secluded, surrounded by water, providing them with a relaxing view and an isolation appropriate to the concentration of training.

The public can take free advantage of the park during the day as well as at night, traversing it independently from the sporting events underway. On this "suspended" level, the collective functions for large athletics events and other happenings are gathered, and here, the close relationship between the park and the city can be understood along the streets and axis composing the "great landscape".

The area, housing a car park for 3,200 cars, will be connected to the green ring of the bicycle path and to the M-30 and M-40. The complex will include 30 tennis courts, a center for high-performance and a sporting center for public use over an area of 174,000 square meters, upon what was once an antique dump. (G.C.)

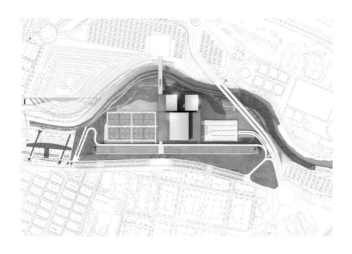

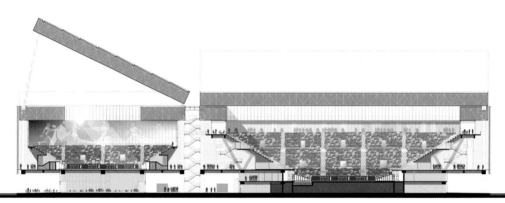

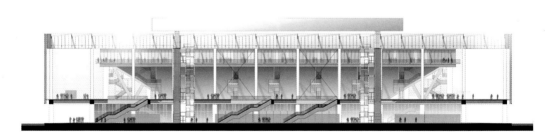

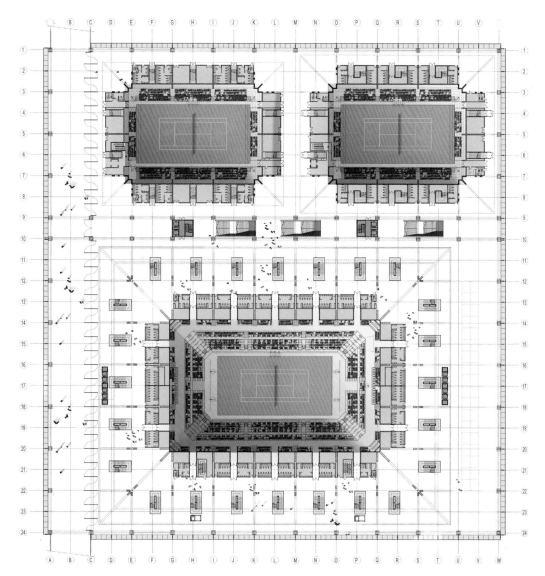

Plan of the Olympic tennis
center

Plan of the Olympic Tennis
Center: rendering of the
main court during a match
and view of the model with
the "convertible" covering

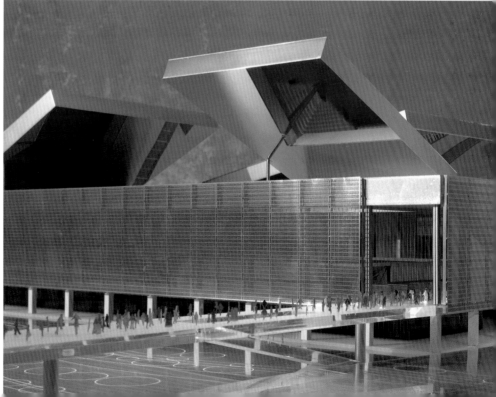

Nocturnal view of the
luminous structure to
house the tennis courts

The transparency
and lightness of the interior
spaces and the distributional
systems

Next pages
The project's
multifunctionality: the
luminous box for tennis
becomes a stadium for
concerts in a nocturnal
rendering

Friedrich-Ebert-Platz
Düren, 2004-2005

In April 2004, the city of Düren entrusts Dominique Perrault with the design of the circular articulation of Friedrich-Ebert-Platz.

This access to the city requires an answer that goes beyond the site itself. Perrault proposes a solution that redefines the identity of the site and the identity of the entranceway to the city, imagining a theatre, a mise-en-scene of nature.

This gesture allows the identity of Friedrich-Ebert-Platz to be changed while conserving the function of the rotunda and of the confluence of the various city access routes. Thus, an open space is created, which liberates a broad view. The slight inclination of the rotunda creates a true theatrical scene, where the spectators, automobilists, find themselves in front of, behind and next to the central scene. The existing trees, exclusively pines, remaining green all year round, are evidenced through carpets of metal mesh, thereby becoming the protagonists of the scene. During the night, artificial light provides a luminous corona around the trees and a distinctive reflection upon the mesh.

The movement of the automobiles thus creates a kinetic view of the carpets, which appear and disappear, shining and sparkling in the driver's field of vision. (G.C.)

View of the rotunda
with the system of the
existing green area
evidenced through carpets
of metal mesh

Biography

Dominique Perrault, born on 9 April 1953 in Clermont-Ferrand, earns a degree in Architecture in 1978 at the Ecole Nationale Supérieure des Beaux-Arts in Paris. In 1979 he specializes in Urban Planning at the prestigious Ecole Supérieure des Ponts et Chaussée, shortly thereafter also earning a post-graduate diploma in History from the Ecole des Hautes Etudes in Social Sciences. In 1981, at the age of twenty-eight, he opens his Parisian studio, followed by one in Berlin in 1992; in 2000-2001 the Luxembourg and Barcelona studios and in 2002, one in Baltimore. Architect and urbanist, with interests in the world of object design (Alessi, Fontana Arte) and material design (metal mesh), Perrault boasts a surprising series of victories in both national and international contests. In 1981 he wins his first competition: the Someloir factory in Châteaudun. In 1984 it is the face of the Ecole Supérieure d'Ingénieurs en Eléctronique et en Elétrotechnique in Marne-la-Vallée, (1984-1987), a work of 40,000 m² that predates by some years his definitive affirmation in the international architectural panorama: his victory in the contest for la Bibliothèque Nationale de France in Paris (1989-1995). From the same year is the transparent Hôtel Industriel Berlier, also in Paris, followed by the projects of the Mayenne Departmental Archives (1989-1993), the Olympic Sports Complex (Swimming Pool and Velodrome) in Berlin (1992-1999), the Centre Technique du Livre (Bussy Saint-Georges, 1993-1995), the Aplix plant near Nantes (1997-1999), the extension of the Court of Justice of the European Community in Luxembourg (1996-2007), the Multi-Media Library in Vénissieux (1997-2001), the stadium of Montigalà in Badalona (1998-2002) and the extension of the Hotel de Ville in Innsbruck, completed in 2002, as is the renovation of Piazza Gramsci in Cinisello Balsamo, Milan. Currently underway are such large-scale projects as the new Olympic Tennis Center in Madrid, the tower of Sky Hotel on the Diagonal in Barcelona, the urban remodeling of Donau City on the banks of the Danube in Vienna, the redesign of the coast in "Las Teresitas" in Tenerife, the development of the north-east area of "Haarlemmermeer polder" in the vicinity of Amsterdam's Schipol Airport, as well as the pluridecorated extension of the Mariinsky Opera House in St. Petersburg and the new EWHA Women's Campus in Seoul. Recently there have also been a number of "Italian" commissions, such as the study for Barilla's new center in Parma, the plans for a system of pedestrian walkways on the Viale della Regione Siciliana in Palermo, the plans for Piazza Garibaldi in Naples,

General Bibliography

with the Line 1 underground station. Strongly interested in a research of planning methodology, Perrault has always combined his professional and constructive activity, not to mention his experimentation with materials, with a profound theoretical speculation expressed and verified both in the process of planning and realization as well as through an intense didactic and teaching activity.

In fact, since 1995 he has been a professor at the Rennes School of Architecture, and in 1997, he is called to the USA, first by the New Orleans School of Architecture and then by the Chicago Urban Campaign; in 1999 he is in Spain at the Escola Técnica Superior d'Arcquitectura in Barcelona; in 2000 he holds classes at the Institut Victor Horta in Brussels and since the same year, he has been among the professors at the E.T.H. in Zurich.

Among the most prestigious recognition Perrault has received, one must include "l'Equerre d'Argent des Editions du Moniteur", "Le Prix Architecture et Maîtres d'ouvrages", the Grand Prix National d'Architecture and the Mies van der Rohe Prize for European Architecture with the Bibliothèque Nationale de France.

He is also Chevalier de la Légion d'Honneur, member of the Académie d'Architecture, honorary member of the Association of German Architects (BDA) and of the Royal Institute of British Architects (RIBA).

From November 1998 to February 2001 he has been President of the Institut Français d'Architecture. Dominique Perrault is presently an architectural consultant for the City of Barcelona.

J.P. Robert, 'Una nuova scuola in Francia?', in *Casabella*, 500, March 1984.

D. Perrault, 'L'atmosphere est a la pluie de meteores', in *L'Architecture d'aujourd'hui*, 254, December, 1987.

A. Pelisser, 'D. Perrault: la matahpore de l'envol', in *Technique & architecture*, 374, October-November 1987.

O. Boisseire, 'A l'alise L'ESIEE', in *Architecture interieure cree*, 221, December-January 1987-1988.

M.H. Contal, 'Hisser les barres', in *Architecture interieure cree*, 224, June-July 1988.

'Dominique Perrault', in *The Architect's journal*, 38, 21 September 1988.

H. Tonka, *ESIEE, Marne-la-Vallée*, photo by G. Fessy, ed. Champ Vallon, Seyssel, 1988.

D. Perrault, 'Dominique Perrault', in *Controspazio*, 2, March-April 1990.

'Progetto vincitore per la TGB', in *Controspazio*, 2, March-April 1990.

C. Downey, 'French Library competition', in *Progressive architecture*, 2, 1990.

M. Rougé, 'Les Hotels industriels', in *Moniteur architecture AMC*, 8, 1990.

J. Lucan, 'Phonemen Perrault', in *Moniteur architecture AMC*, 17, April 1990.

'Plan et arrière plan', in *Technique & architecture*, 391, August-September 1990.

H. Tonka, *Hôtel industriel, Paris treizième arrondissement*, photo by G. Fessy, ed. du Demi-Cercle, Paris 1990.

V. Picon-Lefebvre, 'Du projet architectural aux méthodes d'ingégnerie', in *Technique & architecture*, 398, October 1991.

J.M. Hoyet, 'L'architecture: un art de rangement', in *Technique & architecture*, 398, October 1991.

E. Doutriaux, 'Case Louis Lumiere, Saint-Quentin-en-Yvelines', in *L'Architecture d'aujourd'hui*, 276, September 1991.

H. Tonka, *Hôtel industriel Berlier*, photo by M. Robinson, ed. Pandora, Paris, 1991.

J. Belmont, *Dominique Perrault*, ed. Pandora-IFA, Paris, 1991.

L. Moiraghi, 'Le trasparenze di Dominique Perrault', in *L'Arca*, 46, February 1991.

M. Bedaria, 'La biblioteca rovesciata: il testamento di Mitterrand', in *Lotus*, 70, 1991.

M.C. Loriers, 'Residenze a Saint-Quentin-en-Yvelines', in *Bauwelt*, 28-29, July 1992.

P. Zoffoli, 'Edificio industriale in Parigi', in *L'industria delle costruzioni*, 243, January 1992.

C.A. Boyer, 'Le projet, acte fondateur', in *L'Architecture d'aujourd'hui*, 282, September 1992.

J.F. Pousse, 'Français à Berlin', in *Technique & architecture*, 409, 1993.

F. Lambert, 'Shangai: carre d'as', in *D'architectures*, 33, March 1993.

T. Ballu, 'Nantes: Perrault a dose homeopathique', in *Quaderns*, 34, April 1993.

D. Colafranceschi, 'Architetture di facciata', in *Controspazio*, 6, June 1993.

J. Lucan, 'Bordeaux, un plan pour les deux rives', in Moniteur architecture AMC, 42/43, June-July 1993.

F. Rambert, 'En plein cœur de Salzbourg', in D'architectures, 48, September 1994.

F. Zagari, 'Perrault a Bordeaux – progetto di riqualificazione urbana per le due rive della Garonna', in L'Arca, 87, November 1994.

D.O. Mandrelli, 'Sotto il grande giardino dei meli', in L'Arca, 81, April 1994.

G. Pace, 'Archivi Dipartimentali delle Mayenne', in L'Arca, 86, October 1994.

F. Irace, 'Bibliothèque de France', in Abitare, 330, 1994.

J.F. Pousse, 'Reflets: usine de traitement des eaux, Ivry', in Technique & architecture, 413, April-May 1994.

M.C. Loriers, 'Panorama', in Technique & architecture, 412, March 1994.

D.O. Mandrelli, 'La fabbrica dell'acqua', in L'Arca, 88, December 1994.

AA.VV., Dominique Perrault, ed. Arc-en-Rêve, Bordeaux-Birkhäuser – Verlag für Architektur, Basel-Boston-Berlin, 1994.

AA.VV., Dominique Perrault, Artémis, London, 1994.

Velodrome and Swimming Hall, OSB Sportstättenbauten GmbH, Berlin, 1995.

P. Jodidio, 'Le plain et le vide', in Connaissance des arts, 515, March 1995.

R. Slavid, 'The architect of absence', in The Architects journal, 12, 28 September 1995.

C. Slessor, 'Grand Gesture', in The architectural review, 1118, July 1995.

C. Downey, 'The new Paris library reads like an open book', in Architectural record, 12, December 1995.

AA.VV., Bibliothèque nationale de France, 1989-1995, Dominique Perrault architecte, ed. Arc-en-Rêve, Bordeaux-Birkhäuser – Verlag für Architektur, Basel-Boston-Berlin, 1995.

P. Buchanan, 'Bibliothèque Nationale de France, Paris', in Architectura viva, 42, May-June 1995.

O. Mandrilli, 'Une place pour Paris, une bibliothèque pour la France', in L'Arca, 95, July-August 1995.

B. Houzelle, 'Stratifications spatiales', in Technique & architecture, 418, February-March 1995.

J.F. Pousse, 'Trois lectures', in Technique & architecture, 420, June-July 1995.

E. Alain-Dupré, 'Des lectures et des livées', in Moniteur architecture AMC, 60, April 1995.

J. Lucan, 'La Bibliothèque Nationale de France. Une monumentalité ancrée dans l'essential', in Moniteur architecture AMC, 60, April 1995.

'Bibliothèque Nationale de France', in Moniteur architecture AMC, 67, November 1995.

O. Fillion, 'Dominique Perrault. The national Library of France', in A+U, 10, October 1996.

J. Lucan, 'A simplicidade aparente oculta os esforcos de uma arcquitetura que encara a realidade da material bruta', in Projeto design, 199, August 1996.

Le mobilier de la Bibliothèque nationale de France, ed. Sens & Tonka, Paris, 1996.

AA.VV., Dominique Perrault, Ades East Galerie und Architekforum Berlin, ed. Sens & Tonka, Paris, 1996.

Dominique Perrault, "Des natures", Edition Architekturgalerie, Luzern-Birkhäuser – Verlag für Architektur, Basel-Boston-Berlin, 1996.

E. Cardani, 'Centre Technique du Livre, Marne-la-Vallée', in L'Arca, 100, January 1996.

E. Cardani, 'The Greenhouse Museum, Paris', in L'Arca, 107, September 1996.

D. Perrault, 'Volumes de riserva. Centro Tecnico del libro, Marne-la-Vallée', in Architectura viva, 46, January-February 1996.

'Centre Tehnique du livre à Bussy-Saint Georges', in Moniteur architecture AMC, 70, 1996.

'Biblioteca nazionale francese, Parigi', in Domus, 793, May 1997.

C. Paganelli, 'La città nella città', in L'Arca Plus, 114, 1997.

D. Perrault, 'À propos de ville', in Technique & architecture, 429, December-January 1996-1997.

A. Gubitosi, 'Ampliamento dell'Hotel du Department de la Meuse', in L'Arca, 116, June 1997.

J.P. Robert, 'BNF depart, (bis)', in L'Architecture d'aujourd'hui, 309, February 1997.

Dominique Perrault, Gaëlle Lauriot-Prèvost, Meubles et Tapisseries, Furniture and Fabrics- Möbel und Wandbehänge, Birkhäuser – Verlag Für Architektur, Basel-Boston-Berlin, 1997.

'What is ecology to you?', in A+U, 320, 1997.

M.A. Arnaboldi, 'Un segno sorprendente', in L'Arca, 120, November 1997.

B. Loyer, 'Monument et memoire en reseau: la Bibliothèque Nationale de France', in Technique & architecture, 430, February-March 1997.

M. Ritzenhofen, 'Der Bau: Perraults Nationalbibliothek', in Architekt, 3, March 1997.

M. Levi, 'Architectuur is geen boek. Dominique Perrault. Biblioteque de France', in Archis, 8, August 1997.

D. Perrault, 'Umbruch im Steinbruch', in Architektur und Bauform, 6 (191), November-December 1997.

T. Vidler, 'Arte/Architettura: nuova mobilità delle istituzioni', in Lotus, 95, December 1997.

R. Raderschall, 'A new 'nature in the town'', in Anthos, 1, 1998.

F. Rambert, D'architectures, 82, April 1998.

Petits projets, Edizioni G. Gili SA, Barcelona, 1998.

AA. VV., Dominique Perrault 'Des Natures', catalog of the exhibit in the Gallery TN Probe Tokyo, ed. Masayuki Fuchigami, Tokyo, 1998.

'Olympic Velodrome', in A+U, 335, June 1998.

I Dominique Perrault Sted, catalog of the exhibit at the Danish Center for Architecture in Copenhagen, ed. E. Messerschmidt & G. Hansen, 1998.

L'Hôpital du livre – Centre technique de la Bibliothèque

nationale de France, Ed. Sens & Tonka, Paris, 1998.
C. Desmoulins, 'Aplix, Le Cellier', in Architecture interieure cree, 288, 1999.
S. Redecke, 'Velodromo, Berlino', in Domus, 812, February 1999.
L. Dammand Lund, 'Arkitekten', 2, January 1999.
S. Manna, 'Velodromo e piscina a Berlino', in L'industria delle costruzioni, 329, March 1999.
A. Rocca, 'X-files: oggetti non identificati sul pianeta architettura', in Lotus, 100, March 1999.
'Dominique Perrault', in GA document, 58, April 1999.
AA.VV., With, Dominique Perrault Architecto, Edizioni Actar, Barcelona 1999.
'Dominique Perrault', in L'Arca Plus, 20, l'Arca Edizioni, Milan, 1999.
'Materia e materiali: una conversazione di Dominique Perrault e Xavier Gonzalez', in A+T, 14, 1999.
Studien aus dem architekturlabor, das innovationsprojekt die 4 dimensionen des bauenes der Pfleiderer AG, AIT Edition 2, Leinfelden-Echterdigen, 1999.
'Dominique Perrault', in A+U monografias, 86, November-December 2000.
F. Irace, 'Complesso sportivo', in Abitare, 393, 2000.
E. Cardani, 'Semplicità colta', in L'Arca, 144, January 2000.
A. Gubitosi, 'Una griglia riflessibile', in L'Arca, 147, April 2000.
'Velodrome, Landsberger Allee, Berlin', in Die Neuen Architekturführer, 22, 2000.
'Swimmingpool, Landsberger Allee, Berlin', in Die Neuen Architekturführer, 23, 2000.
'The Aplix factory', in A+U, 362, 2000.
F. Garofalo, Progetto e destino. Otto architetti per l'ampliamento della Galleria Nazionale d'Arte Moderna, Edizioni SACS, Turin, 2000.
D. Perrault, A. Morin, Aplix, Edizioni Lars Müller Verlag, Baden, 2000.
C. Rutault, catalog for the exhibit at the Hôtel industriel Berlier, 2000.
Dominique Perrault, progetti e architetture, Electa, Milan, 2000.
M. Cannata, F. Fernandes, A technologia na arquitectura contemporânea, Estar, 2000.
'Concorso per l'ampliamento del Centro de Arte Reina Sofia', in Casabella, 682, October 2000.
'Variazioni di scala: nuove costruzioni – Dominique Perrault', in Casabella, 683, November 2000.
D. Mandolesi, 'Il concorso per l'ampliamento della Galleria Nazionale d'arte moderna a Roma', in L'industria delle costruzioni, 345-346, 2000.
E. Cardani, 'Senza gerarchie', in L'Arca, 165, December 2001.
'Dominique Perrault 1995-2001', in El Croquis, 104, 2001.
La Mediateca di Vénissieux, Actar, 2001.
Dominique Perrault: selected and current works, Images Publishing, Mulgrave, 2001.
'Nature-Architecture',
Piscina e Velodromi Olimpici, Actar 2001.
A. Bruschi, Dominique Perrault. Architettura assente, Kappa, Rome 2002.
Morceaux choisis, catalog for the exhibit curated by DPA, Sens & Tonka, Paris, 2002.
G. de Bure, 'GKD 10 ans', in Mesh, W Design, 2002.
N. Coleno, Perrault raconte la Bibliothèque nationale de France, Editions du Regard Scere-Cndp, 2002.
M. Brausch, La grande extension de la Cour de Justice des Communautés Européennes, Fonds d'Urbanisation et Aménagement du Plateau du Kirchberg, Luxembourg, 2002.
M. Vogliazzo, 'Commercio e territorio', in L'Arca, 170, 2002.
Next architecture, 'La Biennale di Venezia', in Domus, 851, 2002.
'Correggere gli effetti', in Lotus Navigator, 5, 2002.
Dominique Perrault, 'Vénissieux', in Casabella, 698, March 2002.
'Dominique Perrault', in A&U monographic edition, 391, 2003.
E. Cardani, 'Vibrazioni metalliche', in L'Arca, 185, 2003.
M. Vogliazzo, 'Come un cristallo', in L'Arca, 189, 2004.
A. Gubitosi, 'Nuovo Centro Pompidou a Metz', in L'Arca, 190, 2004.
P.V. Dell'Aira, 'Centro commerciale M-Preis2 a Wattens', in L'industria delle costruzioni, 379, 2004.
F. Irace, 'L'architettura del Tirolo non è più tirolese',
in Abitare, 435, 2004.
S. Casciani, 'Dinamismo di un architetto', in appendix to Domus, 870, 2004.
'Edificio d'ingresso al municipio, Innsbruck', in Detail, 5, 2004.
J. Della Fontana, 'La strip ipogea', in L'Arca, 194, 2004.
G. de Bure, Dominique Perrault, Terrail, Paris, 2004.
'Dominique Perrault', in WA, The World Architecture Magazine Publications, s.l., 2004.
Piscine et Vélodrome Olympiques, Actar, Barcelona, currently being published.

Works

Chapter I

Velodrome and Olympic Swimming Pool

Berlin, 1992-1999
International competition, 1992-1997/1999, winner project
Date: September 1997 (Velodrome), November 1999 (Swimming Pool)
Location: Landsberger Allee, Berlin, Germany
Client: City of Berlin, represented by Olympia 2000 Sportstättebauten GmbH - OSB
Area: 100,000 m²
Associated architects: APP Berlin (Dominique Perrault, Rolf Reichert Architect R.P.M., Schmidt-Schicketanz and Partners)
Landscaping: Landschaft Planen & Bauen, Berlin
Coordination: Projecktmanagement Olympiasportstatten (Promos)
Track: Herbert and Ralph Schurmann Architects
Sports planning dept: Weidleplan Consulting GmbH, F. Kerschkamp
Structures: Ove Arup and Partners and ARUP GmbH
Period of construction: Velodrome: 4 years and 3 months; Swimming and diving pool: 4 years and 5 months
Program: athletics complex, a velodrome for 9,000 spectators, multi-functional: cycling, athletics, physical education, equitation, concerts and a swimming pool and diving pool for 4,000 spectators, 2 Olympic pools, 1 immersion pool and equipment

Extension of the Court of Justice of the European Community

Luxembourg, 1996-2007
Contest project, first prize
Client: Minister of Public Works of Luxembourg
Architect: Dominique Perrault, Paczowski & Fritsch, Flammang & Lister
Site area: 76,000 m²
Construction area: 100,000 m²
Volume: 380,000 m³

Town Hall and Urban Rebuilding

Innsbruck, 1996-2002
Competition by invitation, winner project
Client: Rathauspassage GmbH, City of Innsbruck
Planner: Dominique Perrault Architecte, Paris and RPM Architekten (Reichert, Pranschke, Maluche), Munich
Engineers: ATP (Achammer, Tritthart & Partner) Planungs GesmbH, Innsbruck
Artists: Daniel Buren, Paris; Peter Kolger, Vienna; Heinz Gappmayr, Innsbruck; Isa Gensken, Berlin
Landscapers: Landscaping Ludwigstorff & Hösel, Vienna
Location: Maria-Theresienstrasse 18, A - 6020 Innsbruck, Austria
Site area: 12,960 m²
Constructed area: 35,200 m² (usable surface), 48,000 m² (SHOB)
Constructed volume: 180,800 m³
Works begin: 2000
Duration of works: 2 years
Program: restructuring (11,000 m²) and extension of the Town Hall (7,700 m²) – offices, congress room, bell tower, bar; construction of a covered commercial gallery (8,000 m², composed of 25 shops from 25 to 2,700 m²), a four star hotel with 96 rooms, a underground car park (18,700 m²) and plans for Adolf-Pichler-Platz

Media Library

Vénissieux, 1997-2001
National contest, winning project
Client: City of Vénissieux
Planner: Dominique Perrault Architecte, Paris
Constructed area: 5,230 m²
Constructed volume: 26,500 m³
Project begins: 1998
Works begins: October 1999
Duration of works: 18 months
Program: reception, reading room, planning of furnishings, offices, meeting rooms, auditorium, facilities, car park. Restructuring of the public space around the multi-media library.

M-Preis Supermarkets

Austria, 1999-2003 (Wattens I, 1999-2000; Wattens II, 2001-2003; Zirl, 2001-2002)
Wattens I
Client: M-Preis Administrative Council
Architect: Dominique Perrault
Location: Wattens, Austria
Works begins: September 2000
Duration of works: four months
Wattens II
Client: M-Preis Administrative Council
Architect: Dominique Perrault
Location: Wattens, Austria
Works begins: November 2002
Duration of works: nine months
Zirl
Client: M-Preis Administrative Council
Architect: Dominique Perrault
Location: Zirl, Austria
Works begins: November 2002
Duration of works: six months

Ewha University Campus Center

Seoul, 2004-2007
International competition, 2004, winner project, February 2004
Expected completion by 2007
Client: Ewha Campus Center Project, Ewha Women's University, Seoul
Site area: 19,000 m²
Constructed area: 70,000 m²
Constructed volume: 350,000 m³
Park area: 31,000 m²
Project begins: 2004
Works begins: 2004
Works end: 2007
Program: University center for approximately 20,000 students
Academic program: athletics center supporting student activity; administration; commercial area; sports area and car park

Landscape renovation: Planungsbüro Decker, Bottrop-Kirchhellen
Site: Jungfernsteig am Ufer der Alster, Hamburg, Germany
Area: 32,000 m²
Program: landscape design of the Jungfernsteig: urban furnishing, illumination, wharf with restaurant and bar, restructuring of the preexisting pavilions, artistic installation

Olimpic Tennis Center in the Manzanares River Park
Madrid, 2002-2007
Client: City of Madrid C/ Guatemala 13 E-28016 E-28016 Madrid, Spain
Architect: Dominique Perrault, Paris, France
Location: Manzanares Park Madrid, Spain
Site area: 16.5 ha
Construction area: 80,000 m²
Project begins: 2002
Works begins: October 2004
Works end: 2007 (26 months of construction)
Program: multifunctional sports complex with outdoor/indoor tennis courts. central headquarters of the Madrid Tennis Federation; swimming pool; tennis school; club house; press center; restaurants

Friedrich-Ebert-Platz
Düren, 2004-2005
Commision: December 2004
Client: Town of Düren, Germany
Site: Friedrich-Ebert-Platz, Düren, Germany
Area: 15,000 m²
Project begins: April 2004
Works begin: November 2004
Duration of works: 1 month

DPA Team, October 2005

Dominique Perrault
architect DPLG – urbanist
SFU

Aude Perrault, architect
DESA
administrative and financial
direction
Gaëlle Lauriot-Prévost,
interior architect OPQAI
artistic direction
Guy Morisseau, Engineer
ECAM
technical direction

Ralf Levedag, architect
Bartlett (GB)
direction of architectural
development
Mark Marten, architecte
DIPL.-ING. (D)
direction of project
management

Giovanna Chimeri,
architect (I)
coordinator of Italian
development
Juan Fernandez Andrino,
architect ETSAM-UPM (E)
coordinator of Spanish
development
Shigeki Maeda, architect
Osaka University (J)
coordinator of Japanese
development
Ségolène Pérennès-Poncet,
DEA Art History (F)
coordinator of
documentation and
research
Anne Speicher, architect
DIPL.-ING. (D)
coordinator of international
development
Jérôme Thibault (F)
coordinator of logistics
Marie- Pierre Vandeputte,
designer DSAA (F)
coordinator of interior
architecture and design

Architects
Antonio Bergamasco,
architect Dr. Arch. (I)
Florian Brillet, architect
DPLG (F)
Francesco Cazzola,
architect Dr. Arch. (I)
Ryo Chosokabe, architect
Tokyo Univ. (J)
Stefan Felber, architect
DIPL.-ING. (D)
Dimitri Goldenberg,
architect (D / GB)
Florian Hartmann, architect
DIPL.-ING. (D)
Kotaro Horiuchi, architect
M. ARCH. GMU (J)
Cyril-Emmanuel Issanchou,
architect (F / D / GB)
Takayuki Kamei, architect
AA. MA. (J)
Daniel Keppel, architect
DIPL.-ING. (D)
Cyril Lancelin, architect
DPLG (F)
Pascal Legrand, interior
architect ENSAD (F)
Michael Levy, architect Yale
University (USA)
Klaus Lindenberger,
architect DIPL.-ING. (D)
Ricardo Lorenzana,
architect ETSAM-UPM (E)
Elena Martinez Caraballo,
architect ETSAM-UPM (E)
Enrico Martino, architect
Dr. Arch.(I)
Yves Moreau, architect MA
CTH (Sw)
Caroline Nachtigall,
architect DIPL.-ING. (D)
Nelly Prazeres-Lopes,
architect (Pt)
Jérôme Santel, architect
DPLG (F)
Eric Servas, architect DPLG
(F)
Tillmann Yorn Hohenacker,
architect (D)

Nina Grigorieva
direction assistant
Chistiane Lajeune
administrative and financial
assistant
Sophie Dauchez
communications assistant
Ekatarina Belozerova
secretary
Raffaella Faccioli
Italian development
assistant

**DPA – Dominique Perrault
Architecture**

Dominique Perrault
Architecture en France
with Perrault Projets
Aude Perrault architecte
26, rue Bruneseau
F-75013 Paris

Dominique Perrault
Architecture en Allemagne
with RPM Rolf Reichert
Architekten
Franz-Joseph-Strasse 38
D-80801 München

Dominique Perrault
Architecture en Italie
with Luca Bergo
Piazza Castello 15
I-20121 Milan

Dominique Perrault
Architecture en
Luxembourg
with Bohdan Paczowski
& Paul Fritsch
7, côte d'Eich
L-1450 Luxembourg

Dominique Perrault
Architecture en Espagne
with AIA, Salazar-Navarro
Plaça de Sant Pere 3
E-08003 Barcelona

Dominique Perrault
Architecture en Espagne
with Virginia Figueras

Avion Plus Ultra
n. 12 Planta Baja
E-08017 Barcelona

Dominique Perrault
Architecture aux Etats-Unis
with Ziger/Snead LLP
Architects
1006 Morton Street
Baltimore, Maryland 21201

Dominique Perrault
Architecture en Russie
with Likhacheva Lyudmila
Ismailovsky pr. 4
198005 Saint Petersbourg,
Russie

Credits